AMAZING

LAYOUT

DESIGN

AMAZING

LAYOUT

Dopress Books

DESIGN

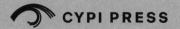 CYPI PRESS

Amazing Layout Design

Author: Dopress Books
Commissioning Editors: Guo Guang, Mang Yu, Yvonne Zhao, Chen Hao
English Editors: Jenny Qiu, Dora Ding
Copy Editor: Frances Moxley Zinder
Book Designer: Peng Tao

First published in the United Kingdom in 2014 by CYPI PRESS

Add: 79 College Road, Harrow Middlesex, HA1 1BD, UK
Tel: +44 (0) 20 3178 7279
Fax: +44 (0) 19 2345 0465
E-mail: sales@cypi.net editor@cypi.net
Website: www.cypi.co.uk
ISBN: 978-1-908175-49-6
Printed in China

Preface 7

Magazine/ Newspaper 9

Book 85

Brochure/ Booklet 149

Poster 195

Others 219

Index 249

CONTENTS

Will traditional media such as paper books be washed away in the wave of digitization, in the same way that oracle bone scripts, bamboo and wooden slips, and parchment disappeared from history? The answer is yet to be known, and only time will tell. But one thing is sure: When we are holding a paper book in our hands and turning the first page, this unique experience — created by its palpable weight, the faint scent of the forest that bore it, its exquisite binding, beautiful images, and amazing layout — is definitely irreplaceable by digital media. Above all, the appeal of the layout proves to be the principal and most essential element. In order to bring about unparalleled reading experiences, designers have connected visual elements and reading content via editing and designing with an eye on details, including sizes, proportions, grids, fonts, colors and other elements of the layout, which ensures the efficiency of reading while kindling pleasant visual enjoyment. Additionally, in the context of the Information Age, today's layout designs have demonstrated even more diversified and innovative features based on the inheritance of traditional aesthetic principles.

This book includes more than 100 choice layout designs by excellent designers and design teams from across the world, presenting layout projects from print media such as magazines, newspapers, books, manuals, flyers, and posters, which are all complemented with numerous high definition images. All pieces included are the latest and most innovative layout designs from across the globe, exemplifying bold and novel styles that mirror the newest design trends and innovations of modern times. In addition to their varied styles, the layout designs in this book reveal multiple origins of the world's leading design teams' inspirations, as well as showcasing their design expertise. This wide selection of pioneering artworks is presented to offer designers, design companies, and design students inspirations for breaking through the restraints of traditional layout designs; these examples will expand their thinking and intellect, and provide a springboard for their creation of unique and extraordinary masterpieces.

Over the past few years, paper media hasn't sunken into a slump as was previously predicted, which gives testimony to readers' and publishers' faithful adherence to and constant favor of the printed page. Therefore, today's designers are expected to assume even more tremendous responsibilities than their forerunners. Designers, drawing on the examples in this book, will be able to recreate their layout designs in terms of content and do their part to constantly refresh print media and enrich readers' experiences.

PREFACE

MAGAZINE

NEWSPAPER

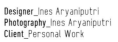

ESC

Designer_Ines Aryaniputri
Photography_Ines Aryaniputri
Client_Personal Work

ESC is a fashion art magazine. The name ESC stands for the word "escape," which means *ESC* magazine is something that one reads when one is bored with daily routines and wants a bit of escape. To provide this, the magazine aims to take the reader to the inspiring world of art. This magazine focuses on local issues and everything about art and design, including graphic design, illustration, photography, as well as fashion and lifestyle.

"**Art** creates *CULTURE.*
Culture *shapes* **values**.
Values **determine** *the* future."

Robert L. Peters

matah ati

Mo rin

Zaz ly

Die

la

Maha

rani

"A **designer** is only
as good *as* the **star**
who **wears** her *CLOTHES.*"

- Edith Head

Kudos

Design Firm_ Matilde Digmann Designs
Photography_ Matilde Digmann
Client_ Personal Work

The design concept of *Kudos* was based on the use of only two colors. This dogma pushed the layout towards new frontiers, and the use of black and white imagery, handwritten type, and pinkish paper became the signature style of the magazine.

Who's Jack

Design Firm_ Sawdust
Designers_ Rob Gonzalez, Jonathan Quainton
Client_ Who's Jack

This project was an entire redesign for *Who's Jack* magazine. Art direction, design, and custom typography were all done by Sawdust.

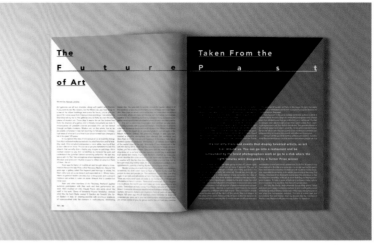

VOLLTEXT — Zeitung für Literatur

Designers_Stefan Zimmermann, Jann de Vries
Photography_Stefan Zimmermann, Jann de Vries
Client_Personal Work

This is the branding and editorial design for *VOLLTEXT — Zeitung für Literatur* (FULL TEXT — Newspaper for Literature), which focuses on contemporary literature. The spectrum of the newspaper covers all literary genres. The focus lies on original articles and preprints of new releases, which are supplemented by interviews, portraits, features, and reviews.

Eine Figur, die sich verrannt hat

In seinem neuen Roman „Die Winter im Süden" thematisiert Norbert Gstrein die Kriege auf dem Balkan und die historischen Zäsuren 1945, 1968 und 1989. Mit Gunther Nickel sprach er über Täterkinder, Autoren als Sonntagsprediger und „die linke und die rechte Scheiße".

Science-Fiction mit dem Kugelschreiber

Der Amerikaner Neal Stephenson gilt als einer der wichtigsten Erneuerer der modernen Science-Fiction

Planespotting

Mit seinem neuen Roman verabschiedet sich Peter Henning von den unspektakulären Geschichten

Lorem ipsum dolor amet

Der Lyrik erster Teil

Ipsum amet sit

Der Lyrik zweiter Teil

Seid ihr alle da?

Paranoia und Misstrauen, Kontrolle und Macht: Philip K. Dick stellte stets unsere Realität in Frage. Der US-Kultautor wäre diesen Monat 80 Jahre alt geworden.

Helden

Martin Gülich liest „Mein schönstes Tor 69/70"

Hier kommt der Debütant

Ein Selbstporträt von und mit Maximilian Steinbeis

Abenteuer an den schroffen Rändern

Raoul Schrott erzählt „Tristan da Cunha oder Die Hälfte der Erde"

Abenteuer an den schroffen Rändern

Raoul Schrott erzählt „Tristan da Cunha oder Die Hälfte der Erde"

Pub Time

Designers_ Sergei Kudinov, Marina Lavrova
Photography_ Darya Gavrilova, Andrey Godyaykin, Denis Gulyaev, Marina Lavrova, Alyona Prisyazhnaya, Dmitry Zdomsky
Client_ Romashka Management

Pub Time magazine is the first magazine about beer culture in Russia, reporting about pubs, interesting pub traditions, facts and news, and good beer. The magazine aims to capture the unique and cozy pub atmosphere. It's distributed through Moscow and St. Petersburg pubs for free. Each issue is dedicated to a certain topic and has a distinctive design. In the layout, designers created bold headlines that attract readers' eyes in the first glance; skillful overlap of the text and photo adds interest to the design. Additionally, bright colors make the layout more active.

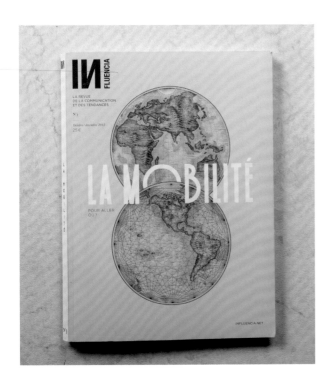

Influencia No. 3

Design Firm_ Violaine et Jérémy
Designers_ Violaine Orsoni, Jérémy Schneider
Illustrators_ Fanny Blanc, Agoston Palinko, Martin Lebrun, Louise Duneton, Joanna Concejo
Photography_ Violaine et Jérémy
Client_ Influencia

The agency designed *Influencia* with the goal of making it a timeless magazine. The concept for issue No. 3 was about softness and sweetness. Designers searched to find illustrators with a poetic style, working in aquarelle or pencil, black and white or colors. The design pursues the idea of being timeless and poetic.

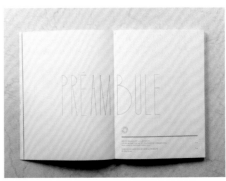

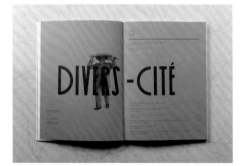

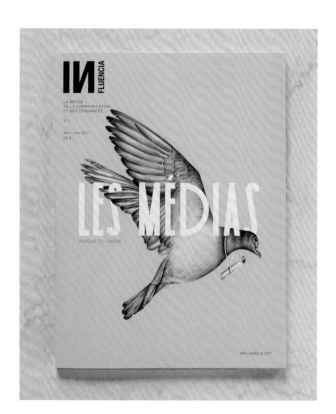

Influencia No. 5

Design Firm_Violaine et Jérémy
Designers_Violaine Orsoni, Jérémy Schneider
Illustrators_Dessins des Fesses
Photography_Violaine et Jérémy
Client_Influencia

Influencia No. 5 was a special project, as it was the first time the designers worked with an illustrator's collective. Also, it was very important to the client for the designers to succeed in creating a design that wouldn't be a reference to a specific time: nothing contemporary, nothing classical. That's what *Influencia*'s design is about: timelessness. Here designers look for unity. Real unity and singularity exude from this *Influencia No. 5* design.

Influencia Special Edition

Design Firm_Violaine et Jérémy
Designers_Violaine Orsoni, Jérémy Schneider
Photography_Violaine et Jérémy
Client_Influencia

This is *Influencia* magazine's first special edition. The designers' goal was to design the edition in a way that consumers could recognize *Influencia*'s style, yet be different. Designers created a special type for the titles, and arranged the articles differently but kept *Influencia*'s DNA: the summary, the editor, the contributor's page, and the illustrators.

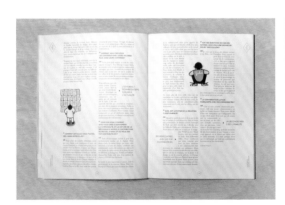

Revista CUADRO

Designers_Fernando Torres Rojo, Saraí Diazgirón Aguilar,
Stefan Ángeles Cruz, Noé Segovia Vega, S. Marylu Aparicio
Chávez, Daniel Zacatenco Guerrero, Vezeta, Lydia Fernanda
Bonilla Maldonado, Carolina Vázquez Polanco, José Arturo
Pagola Trigueros, Mariana Gonzáles Roldan, Valeria Álvarez,
Aniza Fabiola Paredes Lara, Laura Cruz Pérez, Satzil
Alejandra Duran Ferreira
Client_Personal Work

Revista CUADRO is a free thematic magazine, which works
as an official publication of University La Salle Pachuca. It
is created by Communication Sciences and Graphic Design
students, in collaboration with students from other majors,
teachers, and external collaborators. Each issue conveys
different topics and shows different interpretations. Taking the
different features of the contents into consideration, the whole
design looks rich and flexible.

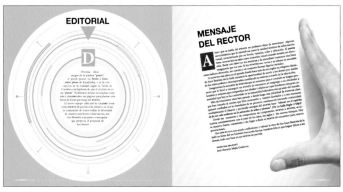

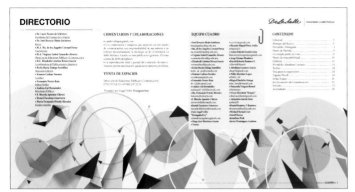

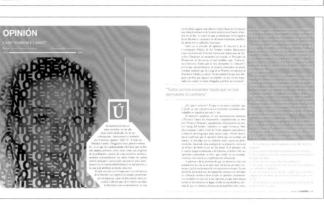

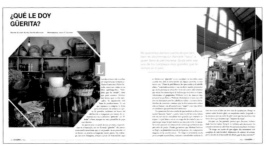

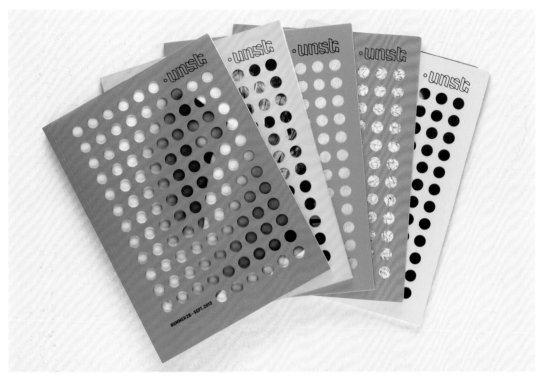

.Unst

Design Firm_HOAX
Photography_HOAX
Client_The Utrecht School of the Arts

.Unst, an organ within the Utrecht School of the Arts, sought a restyling for its identity. HOAX came up with a redesign that structured on and around a platform for students, both digitally and in print. Editorials and a selection of the best work are printed in *.Unst* magazine. In the magazine's layout, the designer used vivid colors as the main tones; the cover is a pattern of die cuts. The overall design is modern and attractive.

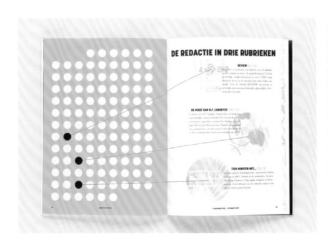

Dark Sand

Designer_Alain Vonck
Photography_Alain Vonck
Client_Bronze Age Editions

Dark Sand takes the reader on a journey through dreamlike, futuristic, and medieval landscapes of early text-based online role-playing games. It is a story of adventurers, dark skies, and tundra. The book is a mix of five-color risographs, and black and white and full color laser printing. Strong colors and flexible arrangement of the text form a free and artistic layout.

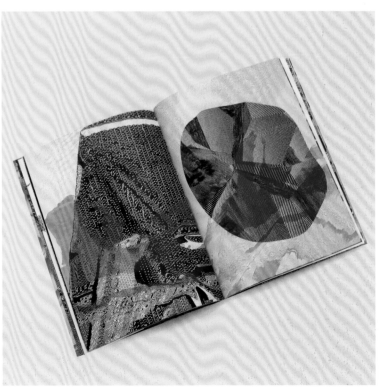

New World School of the Arts Magazine — 25th Anniversary Edition

Design Firm_CR-eate
Designer_Camilo Rojas
Photography_Camilo Rojas
Client_New World School of the Arts

This magazine contains 66 pages; the cover has a squared die cut that gives reference to the 25th anniversary. The four artistic divisions were divided by three-page folded sections that featured full-page photos and highlighted factoids. The magazine is printed locally and published annually in both digital and printed formats. It has a general scope, a regional focus, and it covers a wide range of stories that are meant to inform, inspire and entertain.

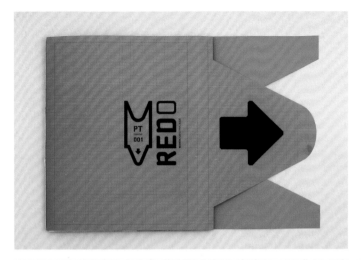

REDO

Designer_Eduardo Rodrigues
Photography_Eduardo Rodrigues
Client_Personal Work

Redo is a bilingual (Portuguese and English) magazine, which covers various topics of art and lifestyle. The main concept is the relationship between the themes and the color red. As Michel Pastoureau said, "Talking about the 'color red' is almost a redundancy. Red is the color of excellence, the archetypical, the first of all colors."

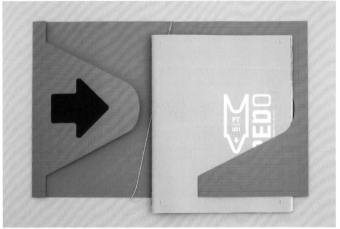

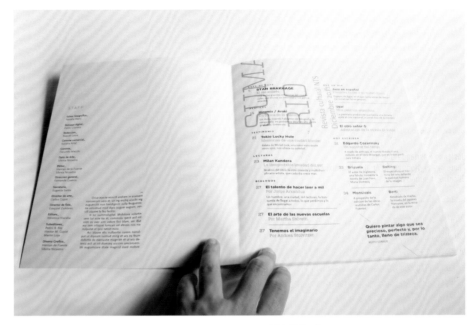

RTSCUL

Designer_Fernanda Cuenca
Photography_Nobuyoshi Araki, Hiromix, Rinko Kawauchis
Client_Personal Work

RTSCUL is a final project for Typography 2 students at the University of Buenos Aires. It's a monthly magazine of culture, art and literature. A container-based grid for text was created, and a floating sub-grid for images allowed the constant play between text blocks and images, between written culture and visual culture.

The III Magazine

Designer_Cristina Vila Nadal
Photography_Cristina Vila Nadal
Client_Personal Work

The III magazine is a biannual publication about the life and philosophy of Christiana, a partially self-governed neighborhood in Copenhagan. The publication is printed in two colors and the layout preserves the Nordic style.

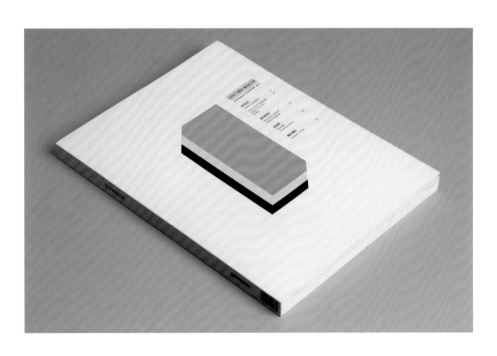

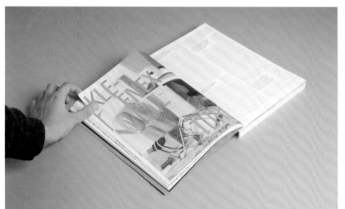

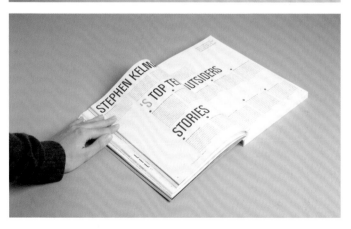

Stuck HK

Design Firm_JKwan Design
Photography_Jason Kwan
Client_Claire Chu

Stuck HK is a magazine-style publication created by the designers in collaboration with an aspiring copywriter, with a timely theme centered on the social phenomenon of quarter-life crisis. With readability being a top priority, the focal point of this design is its reader-friendly tailoring for an easy flow of reading. The design features varying typographic density, accentuated with pull quotes and footnotes, which are all handy visual cues. Each section has a dedicated logo that conveniently indicates its respective theme. Another spotlight-stealing detail is the contrasting yet rhythmic arrangement of text, and the generous use of explanatory illustration.

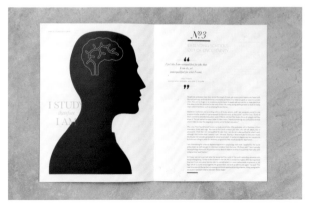

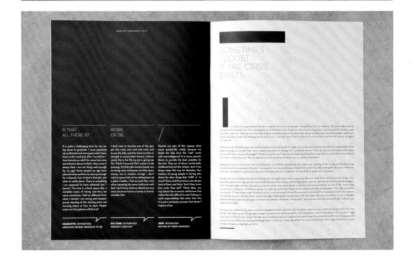

Feeding China

Designer_Ronan Kelly
Photography_Ronan Kelly
Client_Personal Work

Feeding China is a magazine highlighting the key contributing factors to China's ever-growing demand for food. Emphasis is placed on a very confident tone of voice, using textual matter as well as data visualization to highlight problem areas within the subject. In its layout, the designer chose bright red as the main color, which accentuates the book's severe theme. Various patterns were created for the magazine, overlaid with texts, photos, and bold numbers, resulting in a flexible and effective layout.

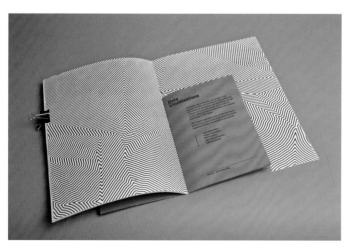

Little White Lies

Design Firm_Human After All
Client_TCOLondon

Little White Lies is a bimonthly independent movie magazine that employs cutting-edge illustration and photography to get under the skin of cinema. Human After All creatively directed each collector's edition cover for iconic impact, illustrating in-house or commissioning world-class artists, including Siggi Eggertsson, Kai and Sunny, Craig & Karl, Michael Gillette, and others. *Little White Lies'* beautifully detailed design stretched the possibilities of print, from wood-carved artwork to 3D treatment.

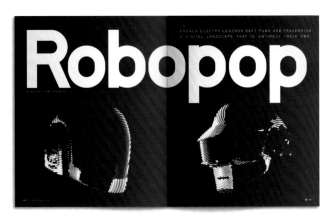

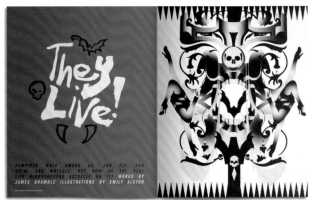

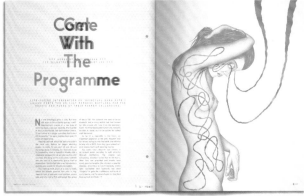

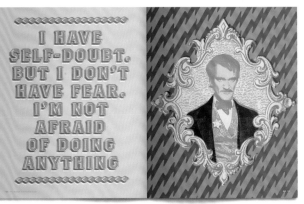

Elephant Issue No. 1

Designer_Matt Willey
Client_Frame Publishers

This was the design and art direction of a new "arts and visual culture" magazine, set up and edited by Marc Valli. In the layout, the designer created bold typefaces and arranged texts freely, which echoes the flow of the photos. All these elements make readers capable of looking at a wide spectrum of things in the world of visual culture.

BIKE POLO.

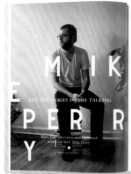

MIKE PERRY

LET THE IMAGES DO THE TALKING

Marc Valli interviews and photographed artist and doer Mike Perry

Brooklyn-based artist Mike Perry is just one of those people. He seems to be able to do so much work, and cover so much ground that, in comparison, one cannot help asking oneself questions about one's own inactivity. It's like being in a vehicle going at moderate speed, and then being overtaken by a very fast one, and thinking 'Have I stopped? Why am I not moving?'

Painter, illustrator, graphic artist, type-designer, art director, author, curator... Mike Perry won't be squeezed into a box. He shows at big galleries. He works with big brands. He does catalogues for fashion labels, editorials for magazines, and ads for software and mobile phone companies. He creates his own products: t-shirts, adhesive tape with patterns, a Mike Perry snowboard for Salomon, a Mike Perry Iron On kit for Chronicle Gifts, Mike Perry cushions, mugs, plates, and even a Mike Perry bandage strips box for Urban Outfitters. His books, Hand Job and Over & Over, both published by Princeton Architectural Press, have sold so well they have been reprinted more than once. He has started his own magazine, Untitled. He has even turned his hand to poetry... And, amid all this, he finds time to reply to my emails – on the same day, as it happens. How does he do it?

NOT EMBARRAS SED, NOT BOTHERED, NOT AFRAID

GOOD SENSE

BAD TECHNIQUE
THE WORLD OF MISAKI KAWAI

Raphael Michelis talks to Misaki Kawai about life, dreams, Japanese puppet shows and Jackie Chan.

UNIT EDITIONS

HOW TO START A PUBLISHING COMPANY

Marc Valli talks to
Adrian Shaughnessy & Tony Brook (Spin)
about their ambitious new venture:
Unit Editions

PORTRAIT BY JULIAN ANDERSON

SAMPA
THINGS TO DO IN SÃO PAULO WHEN YOU ARE NOT DEAD
by Marc Valli

PHOTOGRAPHS BY TUCA VIEIRA

Elephant Issue No. 5

Designer_Matt Willey
Client_Frame Publishers

For this issue there's a colorful bird on the cover, which symbolizes the fancy world of visual culture in the magazine. For its layout, the designer used the typefaces that could catch readers' eyes at the first glance. Well-arranged texts and yellow chapter openers make the design rich with modern style.

PART TWO
RESEARCH
FORECASTS
MOVEMENTS
IDEAS
TRENDS

PART THREE
MEETINGS
IDEAS
PERSONALITIES
CULTURES

THE
MIKE MEIRÉ
FACTORY

BY
KATYA TYLEVICH

PHOTOGRAPHS BY
ALEXEI TYLEVICH

WOLFE VON
LENKIEWICZ

TOM HINGSTON
&
THE LIMITS OF CONTROL

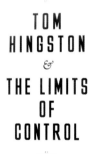

RAYMOND
PETTIBON

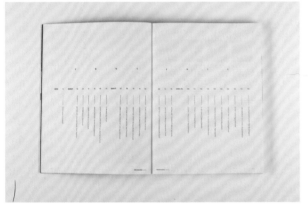

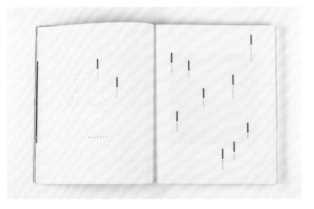

Pure Magazine

Design Firm_Element One
Creative Director_Wojciech Ponikowski
Art Director_Patrycja Dulnik
Designer_Patrycja Dulnik
Client_Finlandia Vodka

This is a bilingual (Polish and English) annual concept magazine of Finlandia Vodka. The magazine includes interviews and articles on art, design, music, fashion, architecture, and the cultural life in Finland. Blue graphics appear in the layout casually, which makes the design concise and flexible.

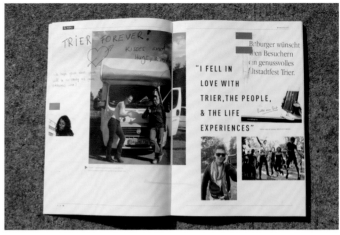

Wanderlust

Designers_Samantha Fine, Jessica Marak, Jared Bergeron, Andrew Spalding
Photography_Samantha Fine, Jessica Marak, Jared Bergeron, Andrew Spalding
Client_Personal Work

Wanderlust magazine is a collaborative travel magazine for students studying abroad. Designers explored experimental typographic layouts and utilized their own photography to fill the publication. The design elements were meticulously planned to best share their stories and experiences of studying abroad in Europe.

überzeitung — Eine Liebeserklärung

Designer_ Wolfgang Landauer
Photography_ Wolfgang Landauer
Client_ Personal Work

Überzeitung — Eine Liebeserklärung, a love letter to the newspaper, was completed as part of the designer's bachelor thesis. The final publication takes the form of an oversized broadsheet newspaper, which is an appropriate format as the project examines the historical and cultural impact of the humble daily. The challenge is the scale of the format — it measures 650 x 1,100 mm, which dwarfs even the largest broadsheet newspaper format. Having such a large canvas to work with means beautiful, big typography can be found throughout its fifty-six pages and column layouts.

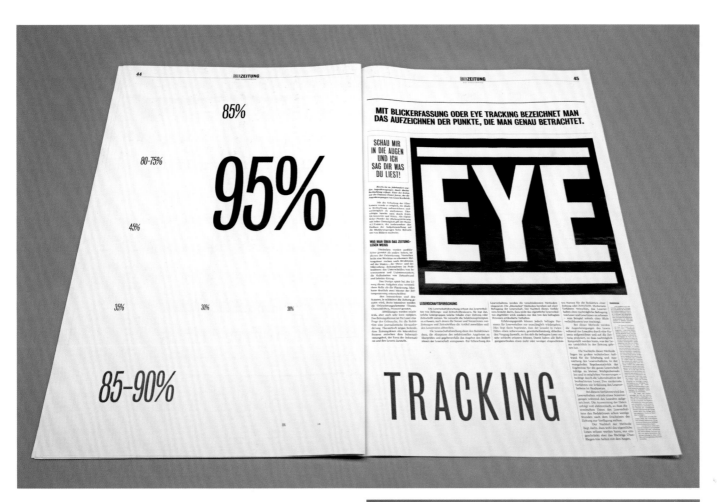

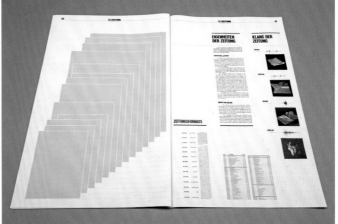

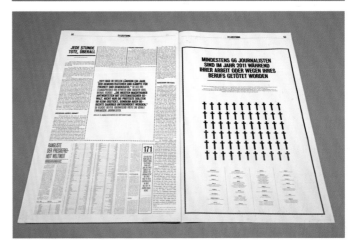

Nya Upplagan

Design Firm_ BachGärde
Designers_ Marcus Gärde, Pernilla Forsberg
Photography_ BachGärde
Client_ Lars Yngve, Nya Upplagan

This is the new identity for the free culture newspaper *Nya Upplagan* (new edition). The focus of the re-design is to accentuate the idea behind the newspaper: to be a truthful and strong voice for free speech, and never to be like other newspapers. Typography and form should, in a similar way, highlight the genuine desire to discuss and question current values, thereby creating an antithesis to the forms that are represented today in newspapers.

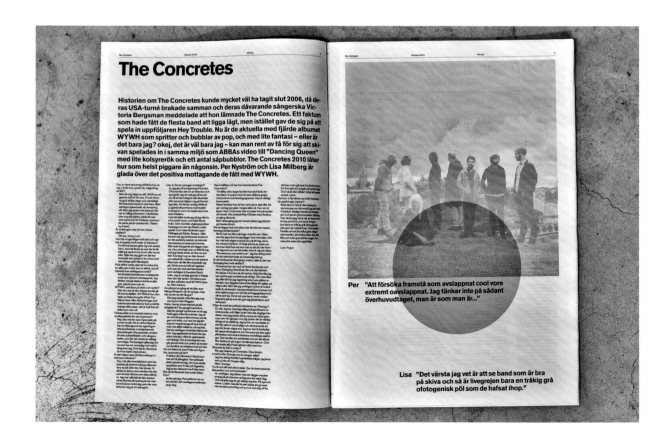

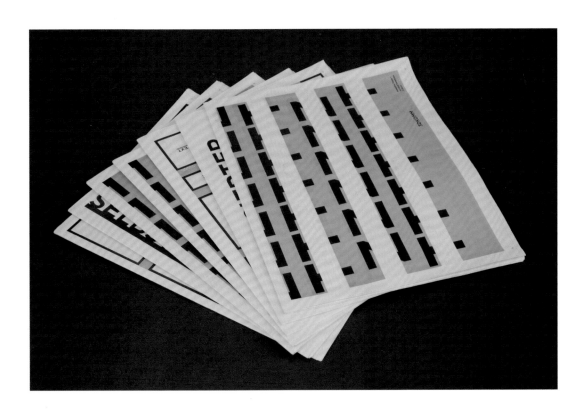

3DKOMM

Designers_Stephanie Passul, Benedikt Grischka, Veit Grünert, Sadrick Schmidt, Magda Zdrojewski, Lea Zier
Photography_Stephanie Passul
Client_Personal Work

The *3DKOMM* newspaper is a medial interface between architecture and design at the University of Applied Science Düsseldorf. It encourages the reader to think and work in an interdisciplinary context. The first issue is based on the term "occupy." In order to interpret the theme typographically, a layout with no negative space was created. The whole journal is occupied by text and images. To take this concept to other media, six typographical covers were designed for posters and banners.

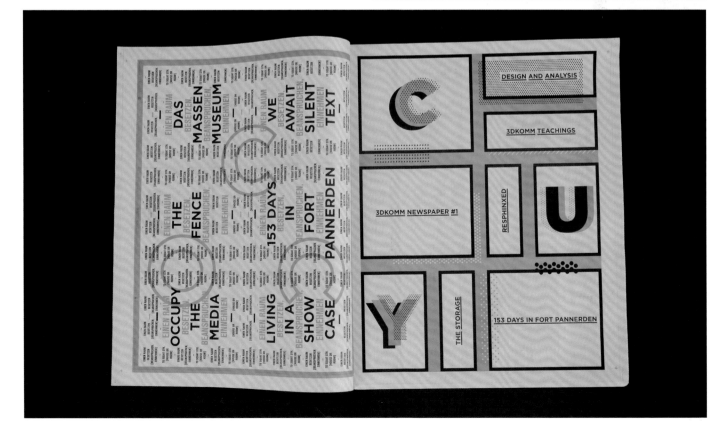

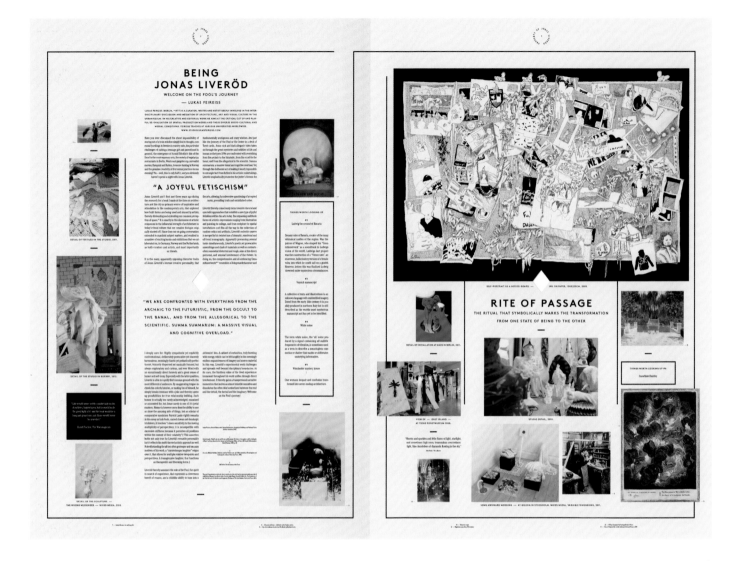

Permanent Daylight

Design Firm_ Re-public
Designer_ Romeo Vidner
Photography_ Jenny Nordquist, Romeo Vidner
Client_ Jonas Liveröd

Permanent Daylight is an art publication by Swedish artist Jonas Liveröd. Re-public designs the publication in a broadsheet format, as a hybrid between a book, a newspaper and a magazine. The publication presents a selection of Liveröd's artistic works, mixed together with inspirational materials, references, notes, anecdotes, interviews and other bits and pieces that form the structure of Liverödland. *Permanent Daylight* has been honored with several international design awards.

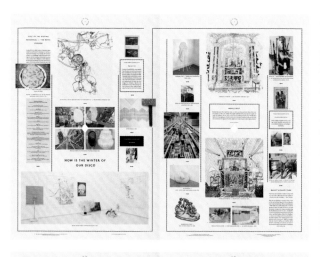

OPERE

CITTÀ
CLANDE-
STINA

MARZO 2012
/ € 10,00

COLOPHON

**Rivista trimestrale
anno X – n.30
marzo 2012**
chiuso in redazione marzo 2012
finito di stampare aprile 2012

direttore

redazione

OPERE

direzione artistica

CONTRIBUTORS

LETTERA APERTA

OPERE 30: Città Clandestina

Design Firm_D'Apostrophe
Client_Fondazione Professione Architetto

D'Apostrophe is in charge of the art direction, the graphic design, and the layout of this quarterly Tuscan architecture magazine. This monographic issue of "Città Clandestina" (underground cities) deals with themes about the relationship between the city, architecture, and territory. This is a relevant topic that deepens the understanding of aspects related to the buildings' construction on local sites. The information in this issue connects the local architecture with experiences of the international cultural scene. The cover of this issue was designed by Gloria Pizzilli.

OPERE 31: Paesaggi al Limite

Design Firm_D'Apostrophe
Client_ Fondazione Professione Architetto

D'Apostrophe is in charge of the art direction, the graphic design, and the layout of the quartly Tuscan architecture magazine. This monographic issue of "Paesaggi al Limite" (borderline landscapes) deal with themes about the relationship between the city, architecture, and territory. This is a relevant topic that deepens the understanding of aspects related to the buildings' construction on local sites. The information in this issue connects the local architecture with experiences of the international cultural scene. The cover of this issue was designed by Bomboland.

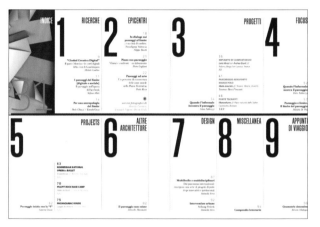

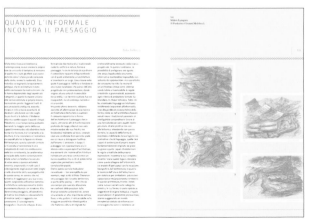

3A IMPIANTO DI COMPOSTAGGIO

PULPIT ROCK BASE CAMP

5B

COLOPHON

CONTRIBUTORS

OPERE

Breviario

Designer_Boris Vargas Vasquez
Photography_Boris Vargas Vasquez
Client_School Project

This is the last project for Typography 2 students from the University of Buenos Aires; it's a magazine about university typographic communication. *Breviario* is geared towards graphic design students. The main concept was to create a bold language and eye-catching headlines to develop a non-traditional graphic design magazine.

Pymes — Constructivist Redesign

Designer_Boris Varga Vasquez
Photography_Boris Varga Vasquez
Client_School Project

This was a project for Typography 2 students from the University of Buenos Aires. The brief was to redesign an existing business magazine with a historical graphic design style. In this designer's case, he had to work in a constructivist style.

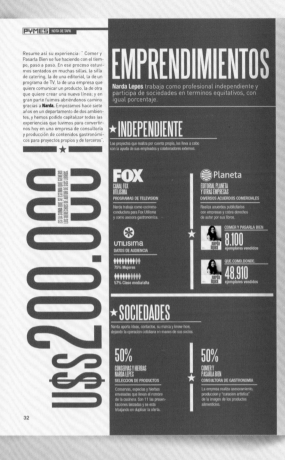

JUP

Design Firm_Atelier d'alves
Client_NJAP

JUP is a monthly newspaper published by the Porto Academy Journalism Center. The artist has redesigned it with the goal of creating a fresh and attractive look to appeal to young people. The goal was achieved by using a dynamic grid, large type, and a lot of illustrations and photos.

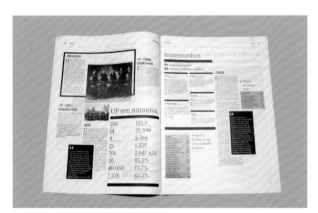

Dramaturgia Contemporânea é o Tema deste número, cujo editor convidado foi Jorge Palinhos. Este extenso dossier conta com entrevistas a vários autores importantes dos últimos anos, como Jean-Pierre Sarrazac, Jorge Silva Melo, Juan Mayorga, Tim Crouch e José Maria Vieira Mendes.

Na secção temática contamos ainda com textos-panorama de Joaquim Paulo Nogueira (Portugal) e Jorge Louraço Figueira (Brasil) e contributos – testemunhos, análises e perfis - de diferentes autores: Armando Nascimento Rosa, Carlos Costa, Jorge Feliciano, Sandra Pinheiro, Renata Portas, Cláudia Lucas Chéu, Rui Pina Coelho, Cláudia Marisa Oliveira, Ana Mendes, e Luís Miguel Gonçalves.

Neste número (Para Além do Tema) damos particular destaque a dois argumentistas: um elogio a Suso Cecchi D'Amico (argumentista italiana que colaborou com De Sica, Visconti ou Antonioni e que morreu em 2010) e uma entrevista a John Logan (autor de vários guiões e atualmente com dois filmes em cartaz: "Hugo" e "Coriolano"). Terminamos com as habituais rubricas de Crítica e Livros.

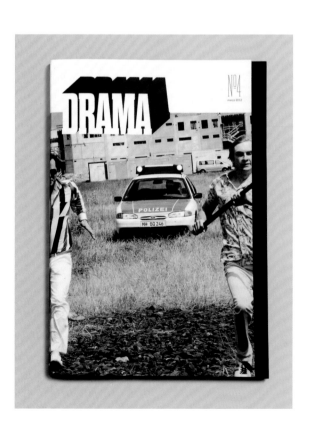

Drama

Design Firm_Atelier d'alves
Client_APAD

Drama is a magazine for cinema and theatre, published by the Portuguese Association of Screenwriters and Playwrights (APAD). Each issue has a main theme. In this issue, designers focused on contemporary dramaturges. The magazine comprises interviews with Tim Courch, Juan Mayorga, and John Logan, and articles covering the Portuguese and Brazilian scenes.

Comunicae

Design Firm_Atelier d'alves
Client_AEFLUP

Comunicae is the monthly journal of the students of arts at the University of Porto. The main issue of this project was to create a visually attractive, contemporary newspaper, but with a small budget. So designers used large type characters in various sizes to get a dynamic pagination and avoid a boring, uniform journal.

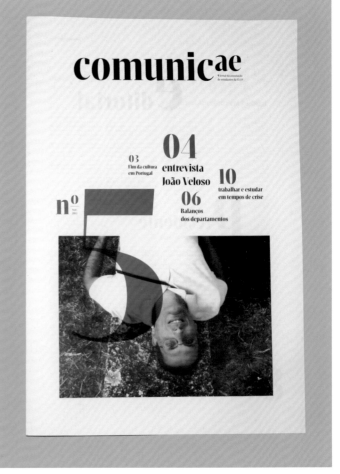

Qualquer Bobagem
Magazine Issue No. 3

Designer_Vivian Lobenwein
Photography_Vinícius Antunes, Amanda Dams
Client_Qualquer Bobagem Blog

Qualquer Bobagem is an online magazine of designer Vivian Lobenwein and journalist Juliana Cesar. Together, they created four issues, including thematic topics and other matters covered in the blog of the same name. In this third issue, the theme is the city and everything that surrounds it, so it includes a cover with a dressed-up dog and a deconstructed fashion editorial with a photo of a model lying on the asphalt.

Dogs in the city

"Sou hiperativo e simpático com todos, mas implico com o carteiro e os garis. Eles me deixam irritado; desconto fazendo buracos".

Buddy, manezinho da Ilha
American Sttafforshire,
04 anos de idade

"Barulho é uma coisa que realmente me incomoda".

Bolota, manezinha da Ilha
Pug, 1 ano e 6 meses de idade

O MUNDO PODERIA SER UMA BORBOLETA...

STREET WALKING

Uneven College Issue No. 1

Designer_Fever Chu
Client_Uneven College

Uneven College is a self-published magazine focusing on different topics: visual arts, design, photography, and culture. It provides a platform and showcase for artists, designers and writers to explore the possibilities of images and text without limitation. The theme of Issue No. 1 claims that "the best designers have the biggest dustbins" that could record the designers' daily observations and experiences.

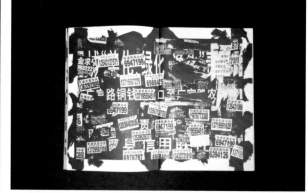

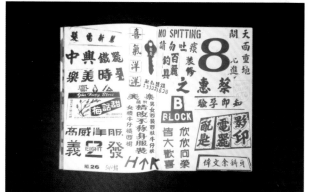

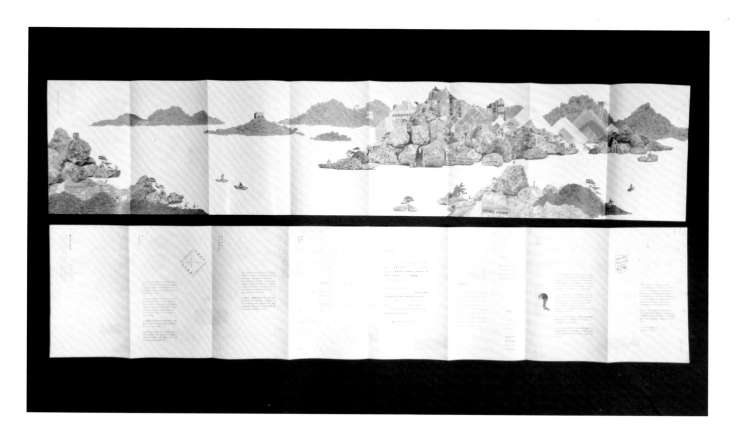

Dale

Designer_Eugenia Mello
Photography_Eugenia Mello
Client_Personal Work

The project's concept was to create a cultural magazine that could be read in different ways without the image or text layers necessarily overlapping. The main body can be divided into two parts — text and visual — each offering a unique way of presenting the magazine's content. It not only proposes a primarily visual journey that allows viewers to interpret, absorb, and travel through the pages, but also presents the articles in text with rich and abstract meaning, which is free of visual interpretation.

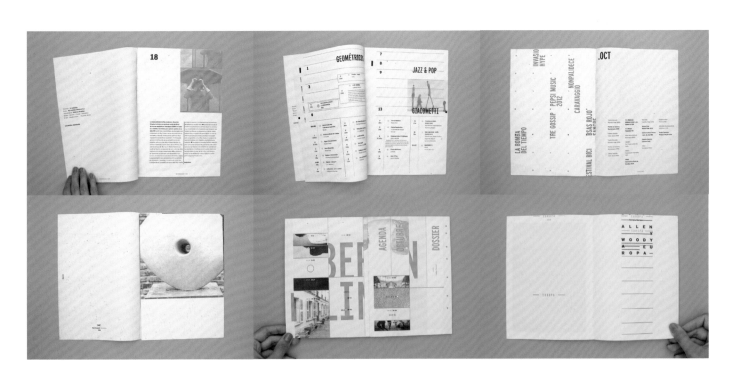

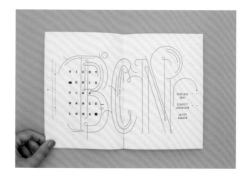

BOOK

Shanghai Ranking

Design Firm_ Sawdust
Designers_ Rob Gonzalez, Jonathan Quainton
Client_ Shanghai Ranking

This project includes book design and art direction for a guide to pioneering global universities titled *Shanghai Jiao Tong Top 200 Research Universities Encyclopedia*. The book is based upon direct interviews with the leaders of the world's best 200 research universities, as defined by the original and most respected international university ranking — the Academic Ranking of World Universities (ARWU). Designers worked closely with research developer Alisdair Jones to realize his ambitious vision for the book.

Atelier Novembre

Designer_Benoît Bodhuin
Photography_Benoît Bodhuin
Client_Atelier Novembre

The task for the designer was to redesign the client's logo, define its graphic identity, and create a book and website. The logo is inspired by the buffer (a tool widely used by architects), and the main design, as seen in its logo, expresses the relationship with space.

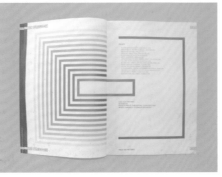

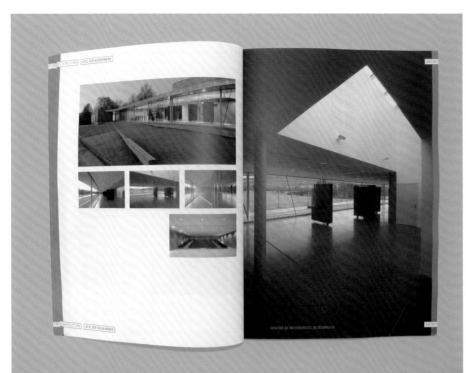

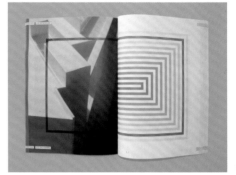

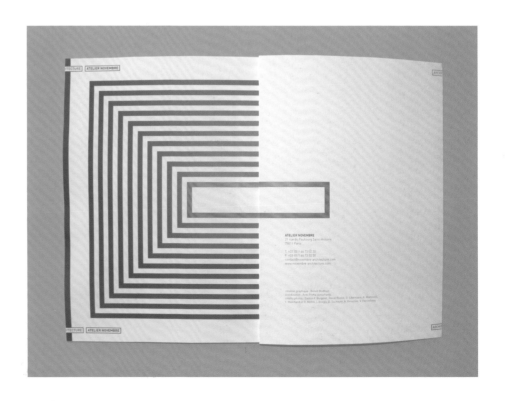

New Frontier Group's Annual Report 2012 — The Missing Link

Design Firm_ Moodley brand identity
Creative Director_ Gerd Schicketanz
Designer_ Nora Obergeschwander
Photography_ Moodley brand identity
Client_ New Frontier Group

New Frontier Group is a network of globally thinking and locally acting IT companies. Moodley designed visual analogies based on prehistory. Significant examples of extraordinary moments in the evolution process of the past are compared to innovative solutions for digital transformations by the IT companies. The concise layout reflects the client's spirit of innovation.

Business model innovation

"Content is king" might somehow sound old-fashioned but for me it is more important than ever. Everything is about creating, adapting and storing information. How companies leverage their information assets will be critical for their future business strategies. Content will be an essential new pillar in prospective business models. It is up to us to create smart connections between the physical and the digital world.

the Homo Sapiens

Our journey

Thriving to become the leading IT solutions company in CEE & beyond

Creation of New Frontier Holding

Business Innovation

The Missing Link Portfolio for business innovation

Business model innovation

Intelligent Portals

Gamification

Intelligent Portals and big data

In the past company web portals have been used either purely for information or as extensions of their corporate IT solutions, i.e. enabling online transactions such as e-banking or travel sites. But most of these web applications treat all customers in the same way and are "just another" front-end for accessing back-end applications. We have applied three principles of social business applications: customization and personalization of the interface, integration of informational, transactional and social content in a flexible way and the use of big data analytics to provide specific customer insights. With this users obtain a completely new experience and companies engage freshly with different client segments.

the Archaeopteryx

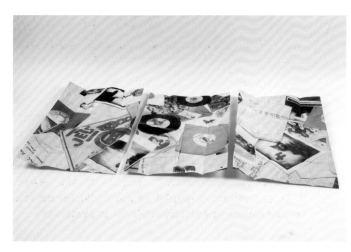

Vinyl Archaeology

Designer_Matthieu Cordier
Photography_Morgane Fleury, Matthieu Cordier
Client_Personal Work

The project Vinyl Archaeology explores the production processes of the album, *Endtroducing*, by DJ Shadow. It focuses on the techniques of sampling (reusing samples of sound recordings in a new composition) and crate digging (searching and collecting sound archives in large numbers). This series of three books interrogates the notions of collection, classification and archiving. These principles have determined their concept and their implementation, both in form and content.

Graphic Happiness Publication 1

Design Firm_ Trapped in Suburbia
Photography_ Trapped in Suburbia
Client_ Premsela Foundation

For the exhibition "Graphic Happiness — 100 Years of Dutch Graphic Design," the agency designed a publication. This publication is about a specific part of Dutch design history. It tells the story of the collaboration between one of the famous Dutch printers "de Jong" and famous designers. The book's cover is made out of five layers of die-cut covers, which together shape the logo of the printer, de Jong. The cover symbolizes the special collaboration between the printer and the designers. The combination of blue and orange makes the page livelier.

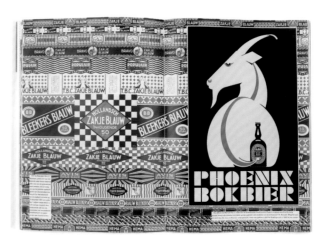

Graphic Happiness Publication 2

Design Firm_ Trapped in Suburbia
Photography_ Trapped in Suburbia
Client_ Premsela Foundation

The exhibition "Graphic Happiness — 100 Years of Dutch Graphic Design" brings the two countries, China and the Netherlands, together; there is an exchange of design knowledge and culture. For its publication, the cover includes logos that are based on the Chinese symbol of "Double Happiness" and the Dutch flag (red, white and blue). It symbolizes China and the Netherlands coming together in design. The succinct and clean layout follows concise Dutch style. It not only catches readers' eyes, but also presents the content in a creative and entertaining way.

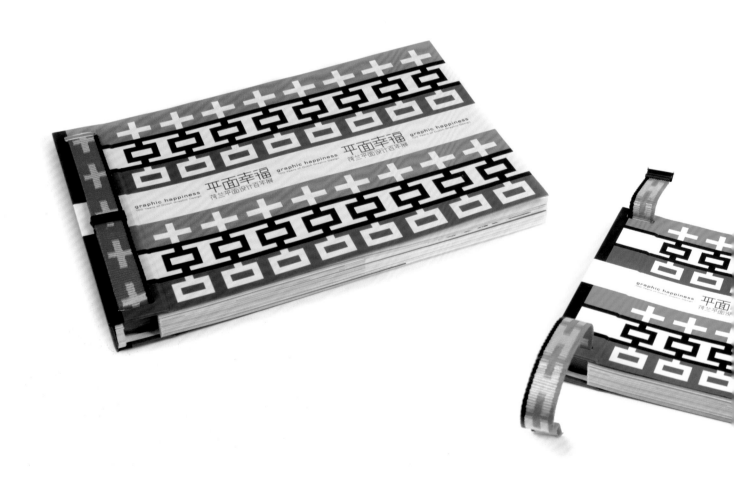

Urban Stress

Designer_ Olga Angelaki
Client_ Master's Degree Project

This project includes both the research and the testing process on how to visualize urban stress for the designer's MA project in Communication Design, all combined into one book. The purpose of this project is to discover and present the meaning of urban stress through situations of everyday life, using simple shapes and forms with a little bit of humor. Image sourcing was primarily done through the internet. Video and editorial design were created, containing all the processes and outcomes.

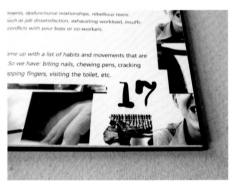

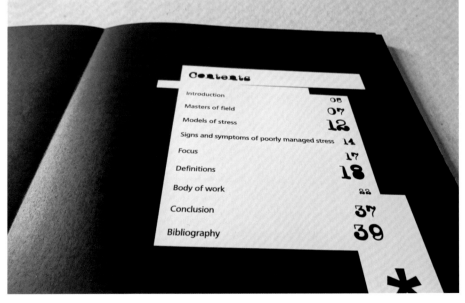

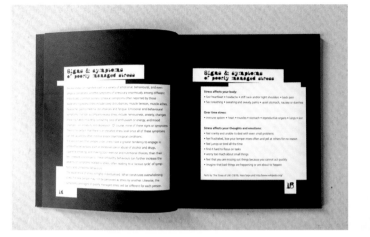

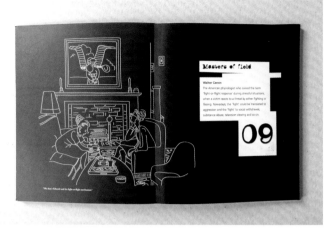

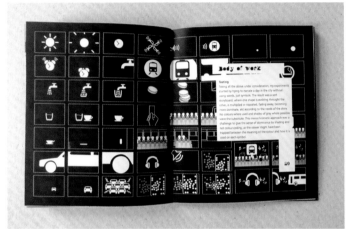

One Year Shipwrec

Design Firm_ Another Day
Photography_ Another Day
Client_ Shipwrec

To celebrate the first birthday of record label Shipwrec (Nijmegen, NL), Another Day designed a book featuring a nice overview of all the quality EP releases made during the first year. Perfectly combined with the features of EP itself, the layout is full of modern graphics and fashion style. Different fonts were used, which not only enhances the book's creativity, but also provides the readers with visual enjoyment.

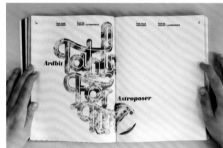

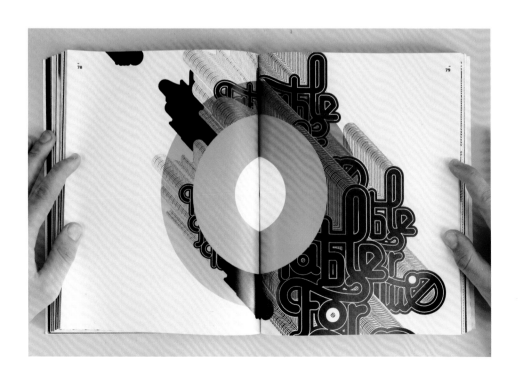

Synchronic Spaces

Design Firm_ Another Day
Photography_ Another Day

This is *Synchronic Space Catalogue Volume 6*. It was printed at the fantastic book printer Lecturis (Eindhoven, NL). A clean and minimalistic book design with a typographic main structure has made the photos the main focus point that highlights artists' artworks in the book.

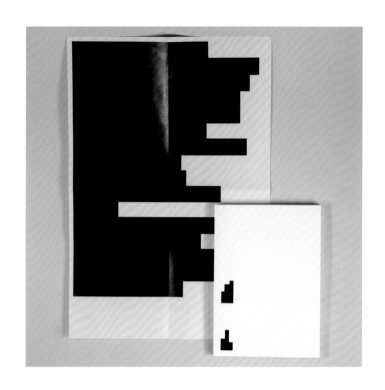

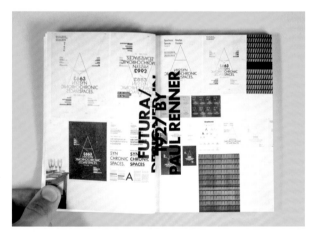

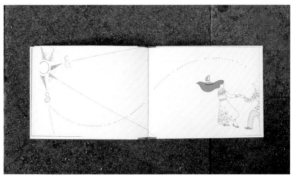

Carrer del Mar

Designer_ Mar Borrajo Valls
Photography_ Mar Borrajo Valls
Client_ Piscina un petit oceà

Carrer del Mar (The Sea Street) is a book where the reader becomes the protagonist. The story describes a poetic walk down a street. The text creates a visual journey, sometimes reminiscent of wave forms. The designer used a limited ink palette in order to afford a really nice natural paper. It was important to take care of the book as a complete piece so that the readers can enjoy the touch as well as the visuals of the book.

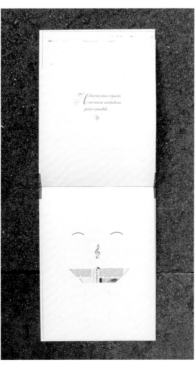

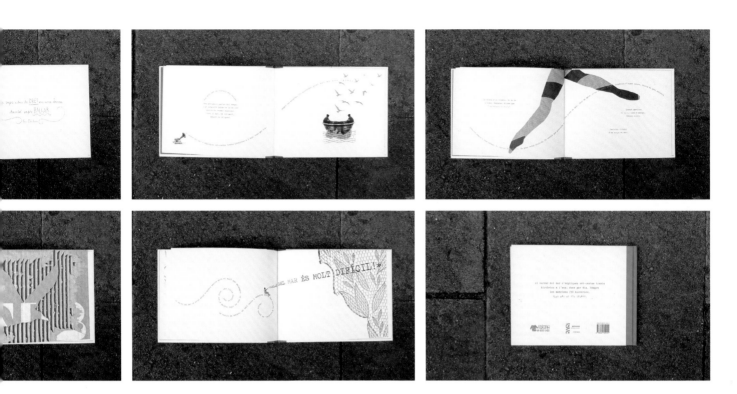

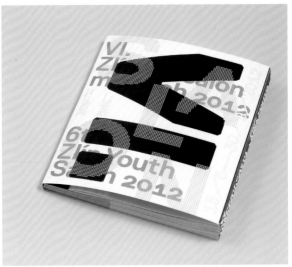

VI. Zlin Youth Salon 2012

Design Firm_Kolektiv Studio
Designers_Michal Krůl, Lukáš Kijonka
Photography_Michal Krůl
Client_Regional Gallery of Fine Arts in Zlin

Zlin Youth Salon is an exhibition of Czech and Slovak artists under thirty years of age, which takes place regularly once every three years. The studio designed a visual style for the 2012 exhibition. On the cover there's the number "30," which indicates that it's an activity among young people. The blue letters floating on the printed materials add vitality to the whole design.

A Perspective on Deconstruction

Designer_ Mariana Alcobia
Photography_ Mariana Alcobia
Client_ Personal Work

A Perspective on Deconstruction is an experimental editorial design project that focuses on deconstruction in graphic design. It explores the use and evolution of the grid system throughout the years until New Wave designers rebelled against it. This allows the reader to become an active participant in the construction of the message. Therefore, this book is in itself both physically and graphically deconstructed, which makes the various interpretations of its content attainable.

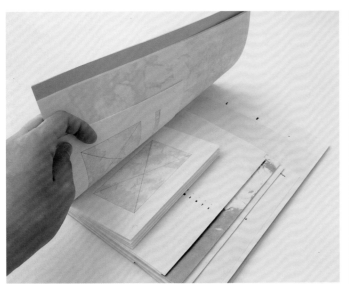

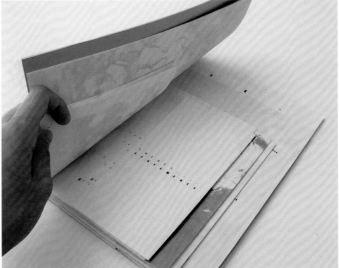

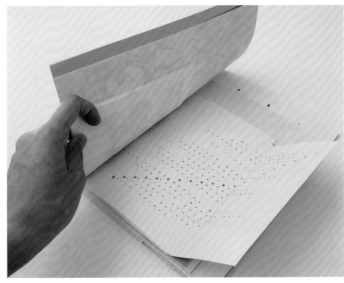

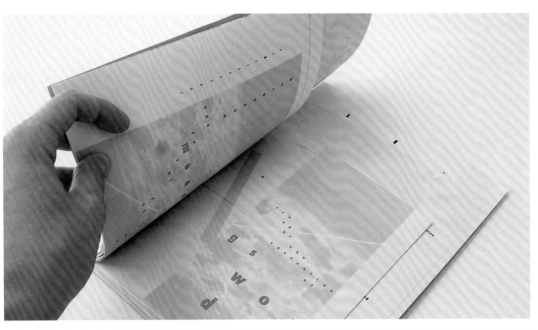

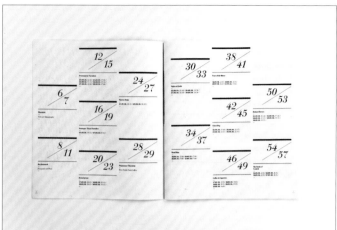

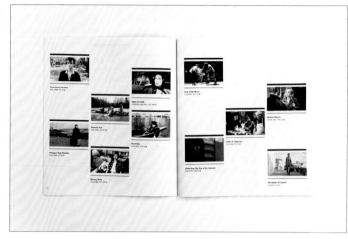

Cinema Program

Design Firm_Grafik und Design
Designer_Ramon Lenherr
Photography_Ramon Lenherr
Client_Kino Studio

This project was created for the introduction of a film director. The dimension of the double-page spread measures 16:9, which in video technology stands for the ratio of the screen. Its layout is defined according to the length of each movie. Hence the longest movie, "Night on Earth," which runs for 127 minutes, covers a full double page. In contrast, the shortest movie, with 74 minutes' running time, occupies a little over half a double page.

BOBBIE:
«YOU ALWAYS
MAKIN' BIG
PLANS FOR
TOMORROW.
YOU KNOW WHY?
BECAUSE YOU
ALWAYS FUCKIN'
UP TODAY.»

PARIS DRIVER: ‹DON'T BLIND
PEOPLE USUALLY WEAR
DARK GLASSES?›

BLIND WOMAN: «DO
THEY? I'VE NEVER
SEEN A BLIND
PERSON.»

NOBODY:
«DID YOU KILL THE
WHITE MAN WHO
KILLED YOU?»

WILLIAM BLAKE:
«I'M NOT DEAD.
AM I?»

«ARE YOU A BUG
BILL MURRAY?»

Coffee & Cigarettes
Jim Jarmusch, USA 1997, 167' E/d

I THINK OF
POETS AS
OUTLAW
VISIONARIES
IN A WAY.

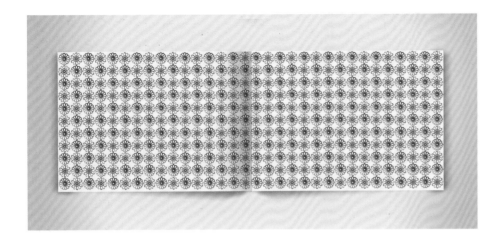

Maestros Tipografos

Designer_Boris Vargas Vasquez
Photography_Boris Vargas Vasquez
Client_School Project

This was a project for Typography 2 students at the University of Buenos Aires. The brief was to design a book about "masters of typography." Boris Vargas Vasquez worked with Zuzana Licko on this project. The book was based heavily on typography; illustration was almost absent. It was designed in a single color.

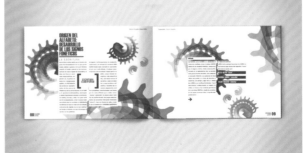

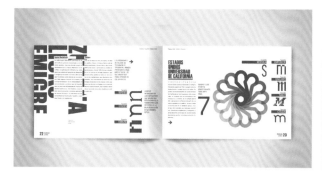

The Erik Spiekermann Issue

Designer_Janick Neundorf
Client_Personal Work

The Erik Spiekermann Issue is a small book about the great type designer and co-founder of Font Shop, Erik Spiekermann. His typefaces are used throughout Europe. *The Erik Spiekermann Issue* features a compact vita which includes an interview about the type designer's life and way of working, and some examples of his work. The front and back of the book is a two-piece cover, which can be opened separately. The book was printed on uncoated paper and hand bound.

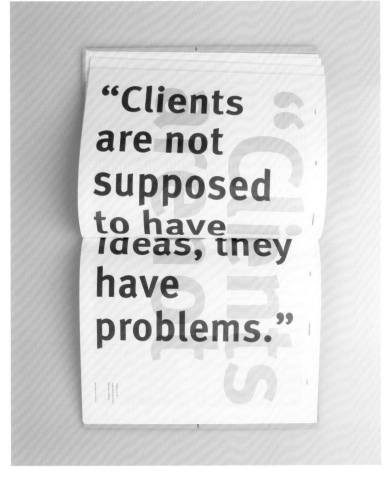

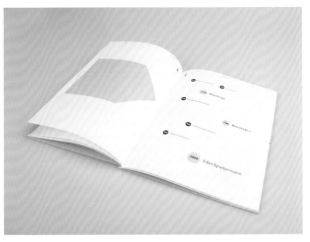

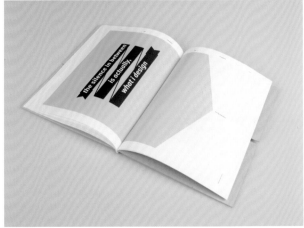

Concise English-Slovenian & Slovenian-English Dictionary

Designer_Tomato Košir
Photography_Peter Koštrun
Client_DZS

The publisher's goal was to contain two large dictionaries in one smaller book. It took the designer a year and a half and forty-seven layouts to design a truly functional yet still handy dictionary. The square format assures the book stays open on every spread. All abbreviations used in the book are easy to find in the front, and irregular English verbs are easily accessible on the last binding paper. Word pronunciations are accessible on every spread.

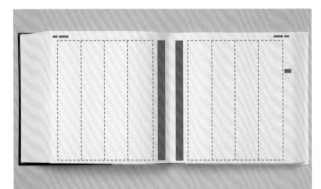

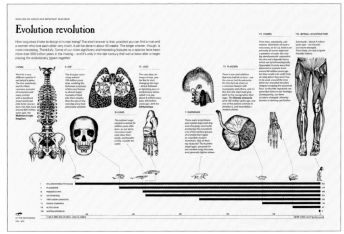

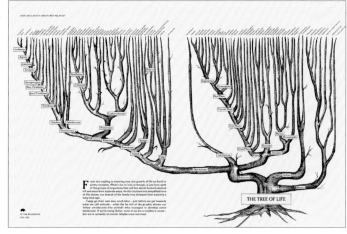

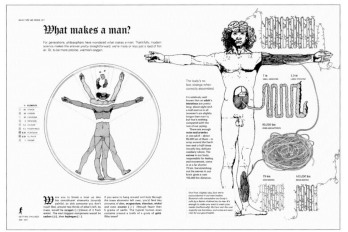

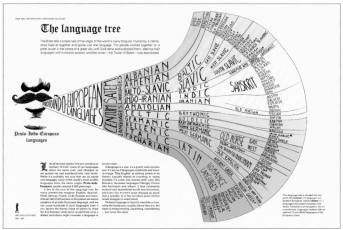

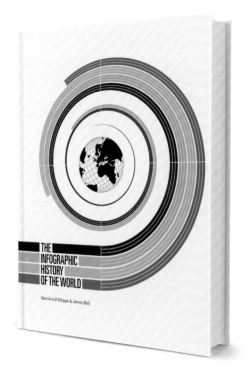

The Infographic History of the World

Designer_ Valentina D'Efilippo
Text_ James Ball
Client_ Harper Collins

This project unconventionally summarizes the history of the world, through more than 100 infographics. A new type of history is here — all 13.8 billion years of it, which exploded into a visually jaw-dropping feast of facts, trends, and timelines. A story of civilization and barbarism, of war and peace, this is history done in a new way — a beautifully designed collection of the most insightful and revealing trends that tell us what the human race has been up to, and where we're heading.

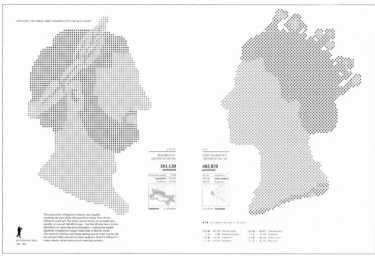

Working men of the world, unite!

Working men of the world, unite! You have nothing to lose but your chains' was Marx and Engels' plea to the proletariat. Had they been entirely truthful, they might have added and maybe a limb or two, possibly your freedom, and maybe your life', but it pays to be positive when recruiting for the cause.

The reality is that revolutions are no picnic: not only do they tend to be violent in themselves, but they're often followed up by some pretty nasty atrocities. It's enough to lead a cynical man to ponder the word: a revolution of a wheel, after all, leaves you pretty much back where you started.

But still, such events have changed the world for the better and shaped many of our modern nations, so here we've compared a couple of the more significant revolutions and civil wars. Death counts have been kept to the duration of the revolution - not any subsequent actions of the new governments.

One revolution isn't quite like the others: England's Glorious Revolution. The silliest, unhappy with their monarch, politely invited a foreign ruler to invade, and discouraged opposition. As he was helpfully married to the current monarch's daughter, once the unpopular king (James II) had fled the novel line could indeed continue largely uninterrupted. A very British coup indeed (and largely bloodless, though it did spark other conflicts).

Others were less fortunate. 19th century revolutions had body counts in the hundreds of thousands, and in the 20th century they numbered in the millions. Whether the triumphant revolutionaries felt their new rulers were worth the trouble is largely, alas, unknowable...

REVOLUTIONS

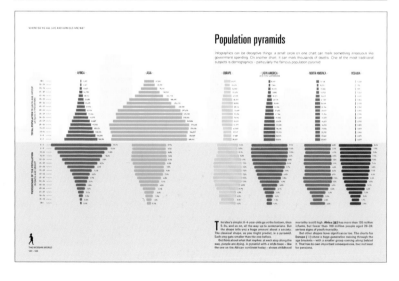

Population pyramids

Infographics can be deceptive things: a small circle on one chart can mark something innocuous like government spending. On another chart, it can mark thousands of deaths. One of the most traditional subjects is demographics - particularly the famous population pyramid.

The idea's simple: 0-4-year-olds go at the bottom, then 5-9s, and so on, all the way up to centenarians. But the shape tells you a huge amount about a society. The classical shape, as you might predict, is a pyramid. Each step gets smaller than the one before. That third about what that implies: at each step along the way, people are dying. A pyramid with a wide base - like the one on the African continent today - shows childhood mortality is still high. Africa (left) has more than 155 million infants, but fewer than 100 million people aged 20-24; serious signs of youth mortality.

But other shapes have significance too. The charts for Europe (right) show a huge generation moving through the age brackets - with a smaller group coming along behind it. That has its own important consequences, too: not least for pensions.

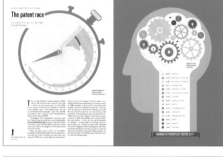

The patent race

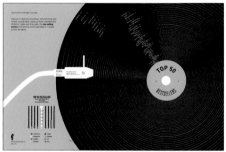

Lock 'n' load

MúzeumCafé Books Volume 1
— Múzeum a tanulóház

Design Firm_Lead82
Designers_Lencsés-Tóth Dávid, Németh L. Dániel, Salát Zalán Péter, Suszter Viktor
Photography_Ákos Polgárdi
Client_Museum of Fine Arts, Budapest

In 2013 the editorial office of *MúzeumCafé* magazine started to publish a book series of the profession of museology. These books are non-profit products and work as a reference for Hungarian museologists, scientific co-workers and researchers. In each book, designers present a contemporary Hungarian typeface. In the first book the designers used a typeface by Márton Hegedüs, called Frustro. This series will also be presented to the public at a large exhibition.

European Culture Programme Guide

Design Firm_DADADA Studio
Designer_Martynas Birskys
Photography_Dalia Birske
Client_International Culture Programme Centre

This project's target audience is young creative people who are interested in culture and ready to spread the European idea. The book consists of eleven different programmes, which could be used as a reference for culture projects and a catalogue for financing them. The design inspiration of the guide was from a formulary book. The novel, bold layout fully displays the creative content of the book.

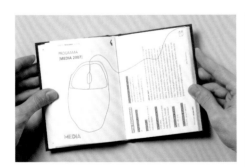

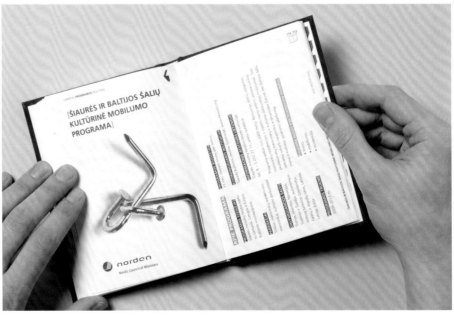

NOT FOU?D

NOT FOU🗵D

И, надеюсь, счастливы... Ну а возраст?

МУЗЫК🗵ЛЬНЫЙ ФОН

LAPHROAIG

ВСЕ ЗНАЮТ ПЕСНЮ ВЫСОЦКОГО: «КТО КОНЧИЛ ЖИЗНЬ ТРАГИЧЕСКИ, ТОТ ИСТИННЫЙ ПОЭТ, А ЕСЛИ В ТОЧНЫЙ СРОК – ТО В ПОЛНОЙ МЕРЕ».

МУЗЫК🗵ЛЬНЫЙ ФОН

013

Спустя менее чем три недели умерла от передозировки наркотиков певица Дженис Джоплин. 3 июля 1971 года умер от сердечной недостаточности Джим Моррисон, лидер группы The Doors. 5 апреля 1994 года выстрелил себе в голову из охотничьего ружья лидер Nirvana Курт Кобейн. 23 июля 2011 года присоединилась к «Клубу 27» Эми Уайнхаус. Большинство летописцев и комментаторов не забывают упомянуть версию убийства, которая присутствовала в расследовании каждого из трагических эпизодов.

014

В списке «навеки 27-летних» не обошлось и без русского жизни. Именно в этом возрасте 17 февраля 1988 года прервалась (и вероятнее всего – по его собственной инициативе) жизнь рок-барда Александра Башлачёва. В его случае насчёт насильственного лишения жизни. И если продолжать в данном контексте русскую тему, то здесь, скорее, впору говорить о «Клубе 37», который ярко описан в песне Владимира Высоцкого «О фатальных датах и цифрах». Правда, Михаил Лермонтов входит как раз в число тех, кто покинул этот мир в 27 лет. В первых рядах тех, кто активно исследует этот феномен, естественно, астрологи. Они, конечно, склонны объяснить эти эпизоды расстановкой звёзд на небе.

015

«Клуб 27» действительно очень удобный сюжетный инструмент для журналистов. «Ещё один вступил в «Клуб 27» – легче всего сразу вписать очередную преждевременную кончину в мистические рамки проклятого возраста. Люди верят в «Клуб», пишут о нём книги и снимают фильмы. Есть несколько музыкальных групп, названных в честь «Клуба 27». В «Клубе 27» Курт Кобейн встречал Джими Хендрикса, Дженис Джоплин и Джима Моррисона в раю, чтобы сыграть Великий концерт на небесах, то есть тот самый Great Gig In The Sky из песни Pink Floyd. На определённой фазе помешательства на тему «Клуба 27» некоторые из тех, кто счастливо прошёл опасный рубеж, начинают ярко вписать последовал Хендриксом и Кобейном и теперь их карьера, не получив должного толчка, идёт по наклонной. Такой персонаж описан в новелле американского писателя Карла Хайасена «Клинический случай». При этом если говорить о Курте Кобейне и его склонности к постоянным рассуждением о самоубийстве, то стоит вспомнить статистику, согласно которой наибольший риск суицида настигает человека в подростковом возрасте. А 27 – это уже не подросток. Впрочем, возможно, всё идёт о молодых людях, которые, будучи подростками и переживая все присущие этому возрасту комплексы и фрустрации, вдруг резко нашли выход своему творческому потенциалу, вдруг получили разом все сладкие конфеты, о которых мечтали ещё вчера, то здесь речь может идти о «вечном пубертате», у юности, которой не суждено закомчиться.

016

Брайан Джонс организовал The Rolling Stones вместе с Миком Джаггером и Китом Ричардсом. Когда ему было 20 лет. Когда ему было двадцать два, первая пластинка роллингов на два месяца

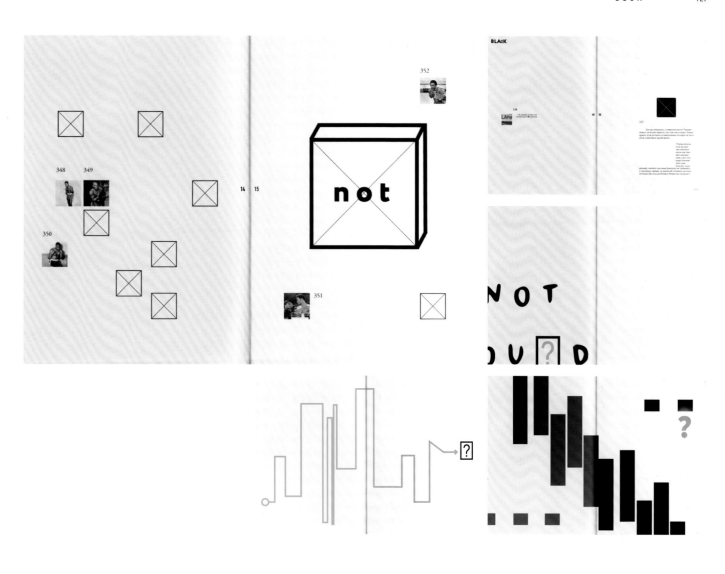

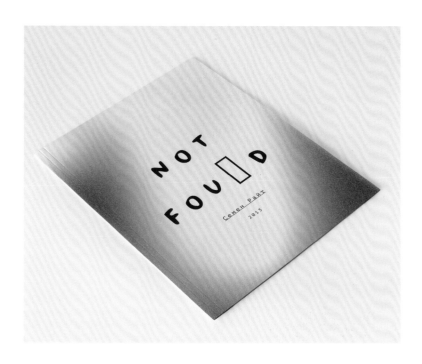

Not Found

Designer_Sergei Kudinov
Photography_Lisa Kondratyeva
Client_M-Media Group

This is a small book of unknown facts from famous people's lives, and it also includes ordinary people whose work has influenced world history but who've been unjustly forgotten. The story itself, the layout, and the typography form an integrated unity. The designer wanted to make readers start asking questions about those forgotten people, to awaken readers' interest in them, so that the important things that are known now could come to the surface and be rediscovered.

Emblems & Gestures

Designer_Brian Banton
Photography_Brian Banton
Client_Personal Work

This is a book based on the exploration of vernacular typography in the Toronto neighborhood of Eglinton West, otherwise known as "Little Jamaica." This book is a companion piece for the "Emblems and Gestures" installation. The exploration was inspired by a passage from Italo Calvino's book, *Invisible Cities*, in which Marco Polo attempts to narrate his travels to distant lands using emblems and gestures. The book includes passages from Calvino's book, hand-drawn sketches, photographs of found typography, and photographs of a three-dimensional structure inspired by the neighborhood.

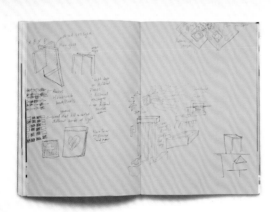

Black Mary

Design Firm_Grafaktura Studio
Designer_Kalina Możdżyńska
Client_Kosmos Publishing House

The book is a thief's love story taking place in Warsaw, Poland around 1920, written in the late 1960's. The collages were made by the authors. Complementary pages with simple vector illustrations and dynamic layouts give a modern look to the whole. Although contemporarily designed, it took inspiration from the 1920's and 1960's art and design. Every spread was individually designed.

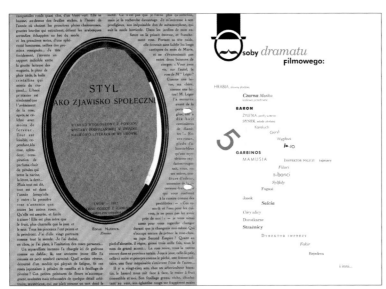

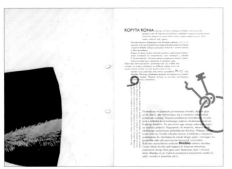

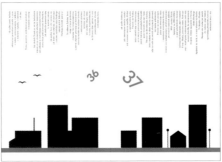

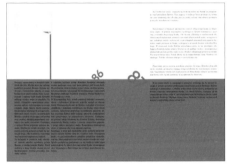

Personal Narrative

Designer_Jonathan Key
Photography_Jonathan Key
Client_Personal Work

The designer was interested in investigating how people demonstrated their heritage, culture and identity in daily life; he was interested in stories associated with these experiences, so he created *Personal Narrative*. In the layout, people's portraits were processed and look complicated, which shows people's confusion and thirst for knowing themselves. Additionally, both printed typefaces and hand-written typefaces were used simultaneously, which shows the delicate relationship between personal identity and social identity.

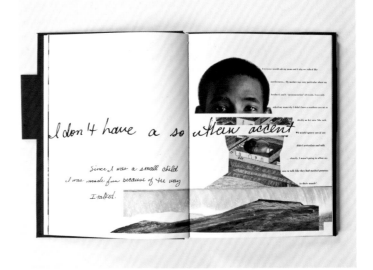

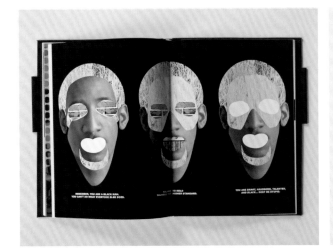

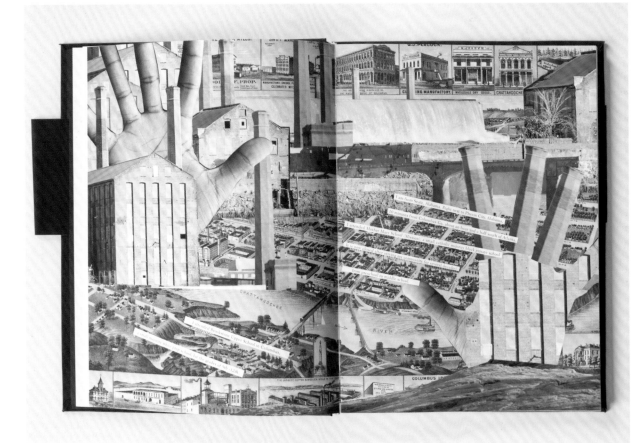

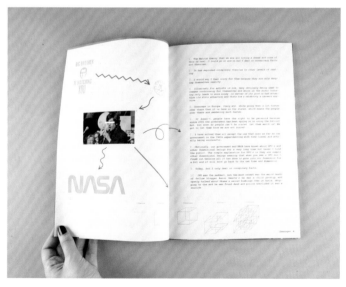

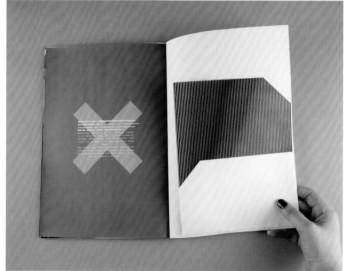

Cloak & Dagger

Designer_Angelica Baini
Photography_Angelica Baini
Client_Personal Work

Cloak & Dagger is a book made for a university assignment. The concept for the book initially came from the designer's childhood interest in espionage and related ideas. She had been researching on how to make decoders, so she decided to give scanimation, or in French, *ombro-cinéma*, a try. To preserve the content's style, the designer applied various signs in the layout; flexible use of overlays and fonts also adds a mysterious atmosphere to the design.

Think Quarterly

Design Firm_Human After All
Photography_Human After All
Client_Google

Think Quarterly is a premium print product; a hardback book packed with cutting-edge commissions by the very best illustrators and photographers from around the globe. Pop-up info graphics, heat-sensitive inks, and innovative print techniques helped to make the book instantly desirable and rich with visual highlightst. With each issue being themed around a single topic, Human After All had the opportunity to apply creative thinking in different ways from issue to issue.

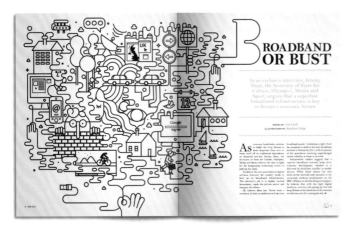

BROADBAND OR BUST

In an exclusive interview, Jeremy Hunt, the Secretary of State for Culture, Olympics, Media and Sport, argues that a superfast broadband infrastructure is key to Britain's economic future.

WORDS BY *Neil Clark*
ILLUSTRATIONS BY *Jonathan Calugi*

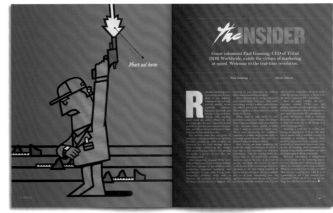

THE INSIDER

Guest columnist Paul Gunning, CEO of Tribal DDB Worldwide, extols the virtues of marketing at speed. Welcome to the real-time revolution.

THE FUTURE IS OPEN

In 2009, Jonathan Rosenberg, then Google's SVP of Product Management and now an advisor to Google management, wrote a memo outlining why open companies would win the future. Today, however, he finds a world that has outstripped even his wildest expectations.

WORDS BY *Jonathan Rosenberg*
ILLUSTRATIONS BY *Nick W. Moore*

OPEN FOR BUSINESS

AFTER CONVINCING THE GOVERNMENT TO PUBLISH OVER 5,000 DATASETS ONLINE, MIKE BRACKNELL IS TURNING HIS ATTENTION TO THE BUSINESS WORLD. IT'S TIME TO OPEN YOUR MIND TO OPEN DATA.

WORDS BY MIKE BRACKNELL
ILLUSTRATIONS BY MIKE LEMANSKI

The Eight Pillars of Innovation

Susan Wojcicki, Senior Vice President of Advertising, offers a Google-eye view on how to stay creative.

WORDS BY *Susan Wojcicki*
ILLUSTRATION BY *Robert Hanson*

Have_a_mission_that_matters

Cognitive Creativity

Do you work in a creative industry? In the digital age, the answer is 'yes', whatever your profession. All you need to do is understand your potential – and then unlock it.

我 这

"但是这个'专属时间'却是在另一个方向盘,紧绷着情绪缓缓在车流中前行度过的。"

THE JOY OF SLOW
慢活 之乐

新闻评论员及专栏记者维尔·墨夫(Will Self)畅谈
为何放慢脚步是获得快乐和提高生产力的捷径。

WORDS BY *Will Self*
ILLUSTRATIONS BY *Craig Wellman*

不

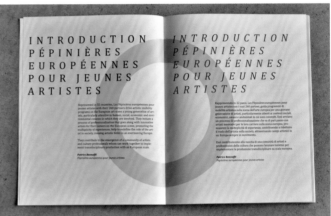

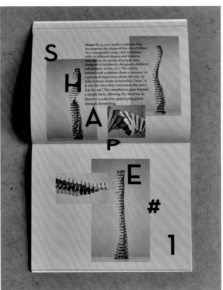

Exitium Milano

Designer_Pau Alekumsalaam
Photography_Pau Alekumsalaam
Client_Comune di Milano

Exitium Milano is a project about destruction of traditional cartography in the city; it is an exploration of new ways to generate city maps and analyze urban behaviors. This edition has been specially done for the "Common Ground" exhibition in collaboration with Klaus Fruchtnis. In the layout, the designer appropriately used lines and figures; the strong contrast between yellow and black makes the design full of creativity and interest.

Hear Our Voices

Designer_Chloe Lassen
Photography_Chloe Lassen
Client_Personal Work

Hear Our Voices is a typographic exploration and celebration of the idiosyncrasies and uniqueness of the New Zealand accent. In the layout, various designs of the fonts and vivid colors highlight the content, which effectively catches readers' interest and helps them absorb key information.

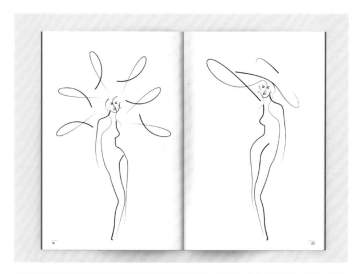

Presence of Style

Designer_ Martin Sitta
Photography/Illustration_ Martin Sitta
Client_ Personal Work

These are sample spreads from the designer's personal portfolio. The book is divided into three sections: vector-based fashion illustration, photography, and ink-brush figurative study. Each spread was thoughtfully designed to create harmonious visual communication between imagery, headlines, and text. The viewer is unmistakably enticed through each section with the distinctive "presence of style" of one person.

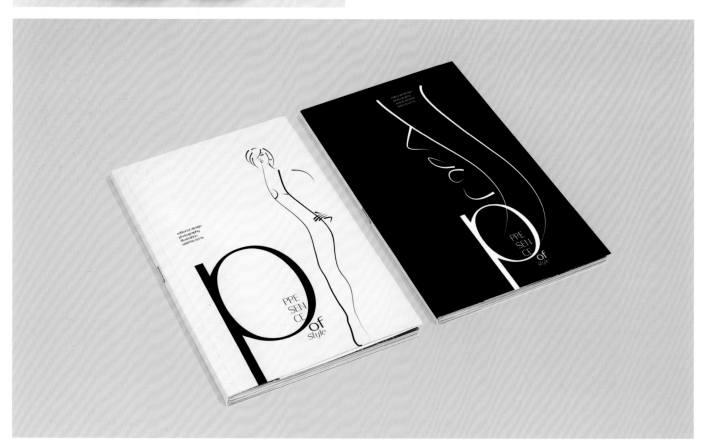

FIGURATIVE STUDY

In autumn, late this year, I was was commissioned to design an overmantel decoration for Nelson A. Rockefeller's New York apartment. The final painting portrayed four female figures, interacting in pairs and grouped on two levels. The present sheet is one of a number of preparatory studies Matisse made between November 16 and December 6, 1938, that work out particular components of the decorative scheme. Here, he depicts two seated female figures from the top section. They languorously lounge on chairs while listening to the song being performed by a woman, not seen in this drawing; in the final composition, the singer stands beneath them at lower right. Reflecting the effects of the music, the women are defined with arabesque lines and graceful curves, set against an exotic background of large fan-shaped leaves. In a separate vignette on the page, Matisse sketchily outlines the form of the mantelpiece to provide a context for the scheme developed above. The drawing is expertly executed in the charcoal-and-stump technique favored by Matisse at the time and frequently employed since his early student years. With this method, the charcoal is blotted out and carefully smudged across the paper, creating soft gray shadows that play against the reworked black contours. Together, these elements add a sense of three-dimensionality to the figures and setting, so unlike the flatness of the finished oil painting.

SO FT angle

2013

CÔTE

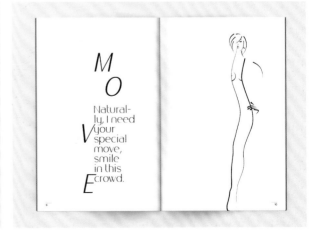

MOVE

Naturally, I need your special move, smile in this crowd.

Unfold Sound of Yoga

Designer_Martin Sitta
Photography_Martin Sitta
Client_Pavla Yoga

The client requested a very clean and contemporary approach. For each spread, the designer created strong headlines, and carefully chose photos that best communicated with the selected letter and headline. Each design element was placed harmoniously in black and white spaces, while yoga poses and letterforms share synchronized anatomy. All spreads were intentionally designed to create attractive compositions for the viewer while the style remains consistent across all pages.

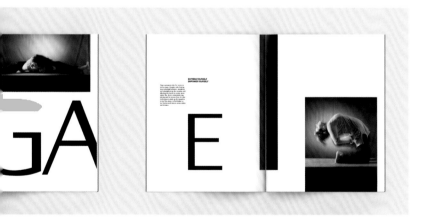

Hundia

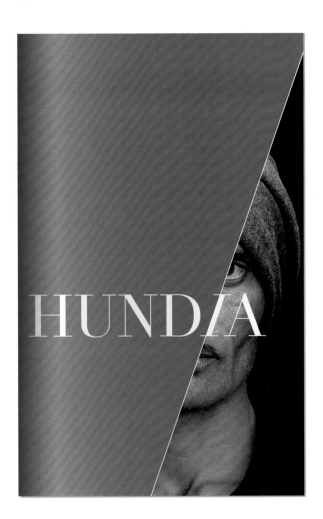

HUNDIA

Design Firm_Kissmiklos
Designer_Miklós Kiss
Client_Gáspár Bonta

For the last thirty years, both Mr. Bethlenfalvy and Mr. Bonta have spent a great deal of time discovering the multi-leveled cultural and historical connections between Hungary and the Republic of India. They managed to establish a mutual interest from both sides through all these years of work, from which this book emerges as a short resume of this wonderful journey. With proper care and appropriate pictures, Mr. Kiss made this into a truly amazing piece of graphic work.

The interest towards India had different sources as well. Indian literature reached Hungary quite early. The Buddha legend got a Hungarian translation from the Latin version called "Barlam and Josaphat" in the 16th century, which has been preserved in the Kazinczy Kódex (1521-1541).

The world-famous Indian collection of tales, Panchatantra got three translations in the 18th century from Turkish and Persian versions but one hero of it is mentioned already in a 15th century Latin text. In the 19th and 20th centuries high quality translations from original Sanskrit tale collections were presented to the Hungarian public. The word "India" was so attractive already in the 18th century that a collection of wise sayings entitled "The Indian Wise Man", or "The Sage of India", originating from a fake "original" ("The Oeconomy of Human Life, Translated From an Indian Manuscript Written By An Ancient Bramin") composed in England in 1751 got translated into Hungarian in six versions from various European languages.

Imaginary "visits" in India occurred in the minds of Hungarian writers as well, from which colourful and popular novels were born: in one of them a travelling Hungarian aristocrat marries a "pariah" girl in an isolated valley, and together they organize a new egalitarian society (Ferenc Verseghy). Péter Vajda wrote a series of short stories taking place in India, among them one entitled "Vajkoontala", relates the tragic love story of a brahmin boy and a low-caste girl, too. Several other 18-19th century "translations" of Indian classics were made trough intermediary texts, like Latin, Persian or English. Sanskrit itself has been taught in Hungary since the 19th century. In about 1750 István Válya, a Hungarian studying in Leiden, met some Indian students there; his discovery of the relationship between Sanskrit and other Indo-European languages preceded better-known works by other European scholars, like William Jones.

The first Hungarian known to have visited India, György Huszti, was not motivated by academic ambitions. He reached the western coast of the sub-continent in 1538 as a slave in the army of the Turkish sultan, Suleiman the Magnificent. Huszti was however a learned man and wrote an account of his experiences, which unfortunately is still unpublished.

#02. Topic

XVI. - XVIII. CENTURY

The interest of Hungarians towards the "East" has a deep historical background, as the ancestors of the nation arrived in our present country in the 9th century, from the East, may be partly from Asia. Already in the 13th century explorers set out towards Asia to find the "relatives", as according to the legendary traditions only one part of the Magyars came to the West, the greater part of the tribes remained in the original home. Friar Julián, a Hungarian Dominican priest started on a journey towards Asia in 1235, and arrived at a place called Magna Hungaria, beyond the river Volga where he really found people speaking his own language. This territory was soon attacked by the Tatar-Mongols, and later no contacts could be found with these "old-Hungarians".

Consequently the Hungarians have always looked upon Asia with nostalgic feelings seeing in every Asian a possible descendant of common ancestors. The great events of Asian history have been a source of inspiration in maintaining the Hungarian national identity and have helped to strengthen the resolve of the Hungarian people in their own struggle.

#01. Theme

MAGNA HUNGARIA

The second Hungarian, who walked two years till reaching India is a real hero, may be the most important "Indo-Hungarian" personality till today: Alexander Csoma de Kőrös.

Alexander Csoma de Kőrös, first great Hungarian scholar of India

Alexander Csoma de Kőrös (Kőrösi Csoma Sándor) (1784-1842) was born in Transylvania in a poor family belong-ing to the military nobles called Székely. According to early traditions, the Székelys and Hungarians were descendants of the Huns who fought both the Chinese (in whose chronicles they were called Hiung-nu) - and the Roman empire, when the capital of Attila the Hun emperor was in today's Hungary. For a nation in the process of awakening, belief in a glorious past was far more important than even bread. Csoma de Kőrös decided to take upon himself the task of giving scientific, 19th century reality to the legend - of establishing the linguistic and historic relationships of his nation, and of finding the offspring of the Huns, that is, the Hungarians who remained in Asia. To be able to travel trough the Eastern countries learned several langu-ages – besides German, Latin, Greek, also Persian, Arabic, Turkish, Russian and English, in the Bethlen College of Nagyenyed, and in Göttingen (Germany), where he studied for two years with the help of a British scholarship.

And even more valuable was his ability to walk long distances, to sleep without a bed or a blanket, to survive on almost any kind and quantity of food, and to value the company of poor and simple people. As without a passport he could not cross Russia, after a roundabout way (via Teheran, Kabul, Lahore and Srinagar), he tried to enter Central Asia by the Kara-korum-road, but he was stopped at Leh, the Capital of Ladakh, in North-West of India.

#03. Topic

CSOMA

It was not the worst place for a philologist to be stopped. All around were ancient monasteries, full of books unknown and inaccessible till then. Their language had not yet been deciphered by European learning. When William Moorcroft the English veterinarian and keeper of the stud, offered Csoma de Kőrös some financial assistance, he happily agreed to stay and prepare a grammar and dictionary of the Tibetan language in the hope that in the books preserved in the monasteries he would find some records about those legendary heroes, he hoped to find.

He found something else – and it was not less fascinating. As he got more and more involved in the study of the language, a hidden treasure-trove of literary works opened before the eyes of the astonished philologist: thousands of unknown Sanskrit works, which had been forgotten many centuries ago in India, but preserved in faithful Tibetan translations. The first eight years were spent in the windswept and snow-covered monasteries of Northern India, in Zanskar and Kinnaur. He had great luck, because he found a real guru who was able and ready to initiate him into all the important sources of know-ledge, hidden not only from Europeans but also from Indian learning.

As Csoma reports, Sangye Phuntsog, a red-sect lama of Zanskar had professional knowledge of Tibetan medicine, astronomy and astrology; he had mastered grammar, calligraphy, poetry, rhetoric, dialectics and arithmetic; he knew the whole system of the Buddhist religion; he had a wide knowledge of everything contained in the books, as well as of the history, customs, manners, economy, and of the geography of the Tibetan countries.

Besides teaching through "shruti" (holy words), Sangye Phuntsog wrote small compendia for his pupil, and whenever he himself could not satisfy Csoma's curiosity, he asked other famous lama-scholars of Zanskar to satisfy the "faringi" (foreign) student. Some of the question-answer books are still preserved in the monasteries of Ladakh as part of the bequest of masters, of the monasteries visited by Csoma.

CSOMA

In 1831 he walked dawn to Calcutta, and in three years his Tibetan-English dictionary and also the first grammar of the Tibetan language was published. Thus, a deed of pioneering significance got accomplished. But beyond this task, Csoma de Kőrös also presented unic treasures of information about Buddhist religion and literature. He was the first to outline the contents of the 325-volume Tibetan Buddhist canon, Kanjur and Tenjur, which described the life of Buddha and the religious tenets that Buddha had expounded. He was the first scholar to publish and translate the Sanskrit-Tibetan dictionary, creating an English version of the Buddhist terminology. If we leaf through the volumes of the "Journal of the Asiatic Society of Bengal" of those years, we will find in almost all of them some article or other by Csoma. They are all of basic importance. Most of the papers were reprinted already in 1911 in Calcutta, and another smaller collection in 1957, and a complete collection of his works in four volumes in Budapest, in 1984. Without any doubt it can be said that Alexander Csoma Kőrösi is the great founding father not just of Tibetan but of Buddhist studies as well.

One more iportant fact: Csoma de Kőrös has to be sharply distinguished from other European oriental scholars

of that age, – as for him oriental research served the deep understanding of all aspects of the culture of Asia, we may say: he studied his own orient, with which he identified himself. He approached the people he studied as friends, stressing the common human values.

After a decade of work at the Asiatic Society of Bengal, Alexander Csoma de Kőrös again set off towards Tibet in 1842 in his quest to find the predecessors and relatives of Hungarians. However, he was never to attain his goal, falling ill and dying from malaria in Darjeeling. His tomb there is now a place of pilgrimage for all Hungarian visitors and a monument of Indian heritage.

Lokesh Chandra writes about the importance of the activities of Alexander Csoma de Kőrös for Indian studies: "He opened up a vast vista of the treasures of art and thought, literature and philosophy, grammar and lexicography, medicine and metallurgy, astronomy and alchemy and other branches of learning of India hidden in the Tibetan language. The darkrecess of India's history shone afresh by the dedicated and pioneering efforts of Csoma de Kőrös."

CSOMA

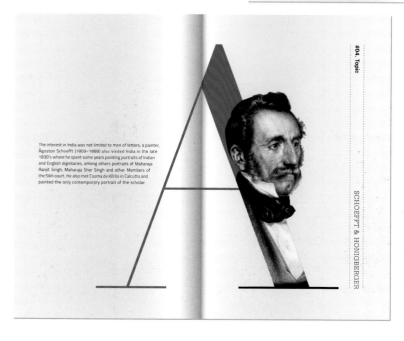

The interest in India was not limited to men of letters, a painter, Ágoston Schoefft (1809-1888) also visited India in the late 1830's where he spent some years painting portraits of Indian and English dignitaries, among others portraits of Maharaja Ranjit Singh, Maharaja Sher Singh and other Members of the Sikh court. He also met Csoma de Kőrös in Calcutta and painted the only contemporary portrait of the scholar.

SCHOEFFT & HONIGBERGER

BROCHURE

BOOKLET

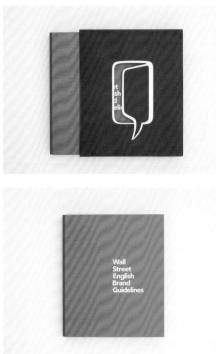

Wall Street English Brand Guidelines

Design Firm_DLVBBDO
Designer_ Luca Fontana
Photography_ Luca Fontana
Client_ Wall Street English

A global brand creates its own world — a world with a recognizable design, a specific vision, a shared philosophy, and a unique experience. In this guideline book, the designer chose red, blue and white as the main colors, which formed an eye-catching and harmonious palette. Additionally, a unique background was created on which the client's name was printed in script form. The whole design is both free and full of corporate culture.

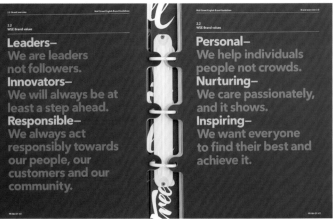

Wall
Street
English
Brand
Guidelines

Spring Program

Design Firm_Matilde Digmann Designs
Photography_Matilde Digmann
Client_Kultur Valby

The main point of the publication is to inspire the people of Valby to make use of the many cultural offers available to them. Each spread illustrates a chain of events within the overall theme: water.

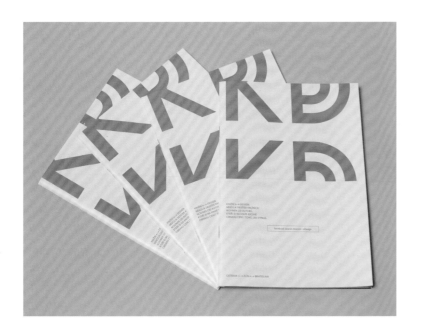

Book Design Brochure Exhibition

Design Firm_ Kolektiv Studio
Designer_ Lukáš Kijonka
Photography_ Michal Krůl
Client_ Kolektiv Studio

Kolektiv Studio organized the exhibition "Book Design" where one can find a lot of new books from various authors; this is a brochure for the exhibition. The activity's logo can be found on the pages, which is in bold blue or pink. Using a black background combined with orange letters or photos, all the elements make the book more creative and eye-catching.

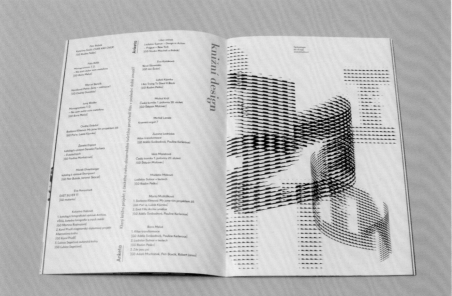

COHDA Commercial Booklet

Design Firm_Chattermark
Designers_Steffi Marie, Stéphane Pouzenc
Photography_Baptiste Almodovar
Client_COHDA

COHDA is an institute of quantitative studies which offers a full range of study for its clients. In this booklet, Chattermark proposes a universe of principles and elements to sign the origin of each production without the presence of the logo. The booklet thus becomes a tool and a vector of identity one wouldn't want to overlook.

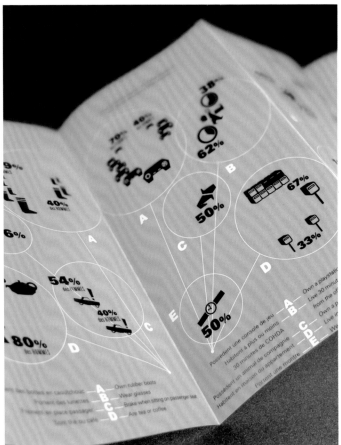

Process/Outcome

Designer_Caitlin Workman
Client_Personal Work

Process/Outcome was created as an exhibition of the designer's thinking process and experimental approach in solving problems. It highlights the design process over outcome, and presents playing as a way of discovering. Forward thinking and experimentation is the course to change perception. The designer chose a creative way to display the brainstorm process: Various typefaces, changeable arrangements, and beautiful photos are presented. All these elements work together to create this book, which faithfully records the exploration of innovative solutions.

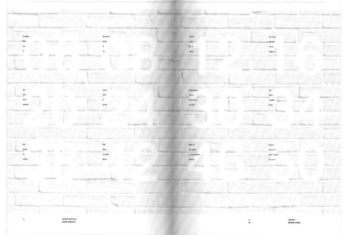

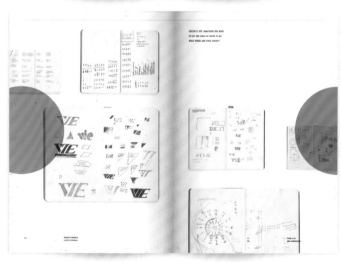

music, clock, darts,
creatures of the lab.

I LOVE IT WHEN I
CLEAR MY DESK &
FIND MY HIDDEN
COLLECTION OF
BONE TOOLS.

Strange
things
can
happen.

03
Go Crazy

SOMETIMES
YOU JUST
HAVE TO
EXPERIMENT
WITH IT...
& AT TIMES
YOUR
INSTRUCTOR
WILL
06   CALL IT   experiment often
POOP,
TEAR
IT DOWN,
& MAKE YOU
START OVER.

BUT
YOU'LL BE A
BETTER DESIGNER
BECAUSE OF IT

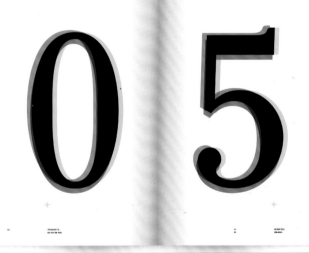

0 5

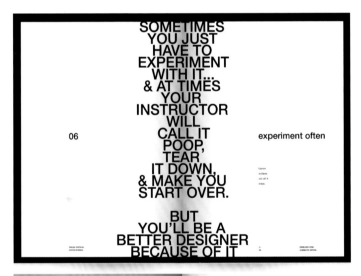

LARGE
VERY
LARGE
TYPE

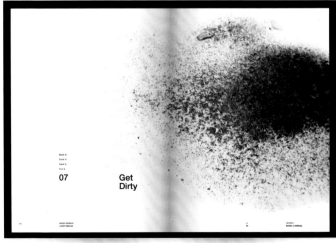

07   Get
Dirty

Political Speech Reporter

Designer_Sam van Straaten
Client_Personal Work

This is a conceptual look at the workings of freedom of speech and freedom of the press in the political sphere in South Africa in 2009. The project aims to question the border between freedom of speech and hate speech.

20 Rules for a Good Design

Design Firm_When Ideas Happen
Designer_Ricardo Vieira
Photography_Ricardo Vieira

This is an editorial piece with twenty rules on how to make a good design, containing examples from well-established graphic designers from all over the world. It includes rules such as, "Use an element that captures the attention in the first seconds." The main idea behind the whole brochure was to have a chalkboard type of layout in which each rule would give a lesson about graphic design.

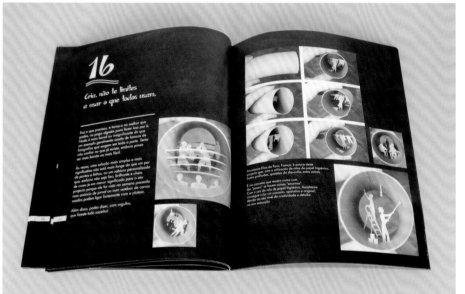

Editorial Typologies

Designer_Boris Vargas Vasquez
Photography_Boris Vargas Vasquez
Client_School Project

This was a school project for Graphic Design 2 students at the University of Buenos Aires. The brief was to design different editorial pieces with the same content about a writer. The forms include a newspaper, a brochure, and a booklet. The aim was to design a non-traditional language.

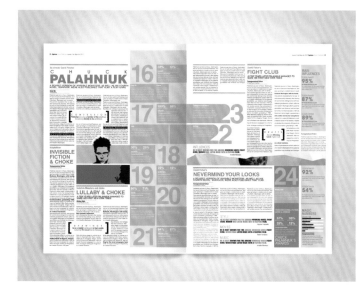

1° Dezembro

Design Firm_ Gen Design Studio
Creative Director_ Leandro Veloso
Designer_ Catarina Correia
Photography_ Leandro Veloso
Client_ Associação Académica da Universidade do Minho

The first of December is the date of Portugal's independence in 1640, after sixty years of Spanish rule. History records that Braga students were the first to welcome the new king and celebrate the restoration of independence. They started a tradition that is renewed every year and still lives today. The concept for the event image was to represent the independence through the cut from Spain. The Gen Design Studio established a clean visual language with color and infographic elements, which were used in all visual materials.

Sports Booklet

Designers_Alice Rinaudo, Chiara Cavagion, Federica Artuffo, Irene Fucci
Photography_Irene Fucci
Client_Personal Work

Two booklets made from the pages of different magazines were overprinted and staple-joined with the theme, "positive and negative aspects of sports." Designers selected among thousands of magazines for pages that best fitted these criteria: not too full, good-looking on both sides, and strong. Then they designed the graphics. The challenge was the understanding of the folding and fitting of the spreads. Finally they fed the paper into the printer sheet by sheet, trying not to print in the wrong direction and hoping the paper didn't get stuck.

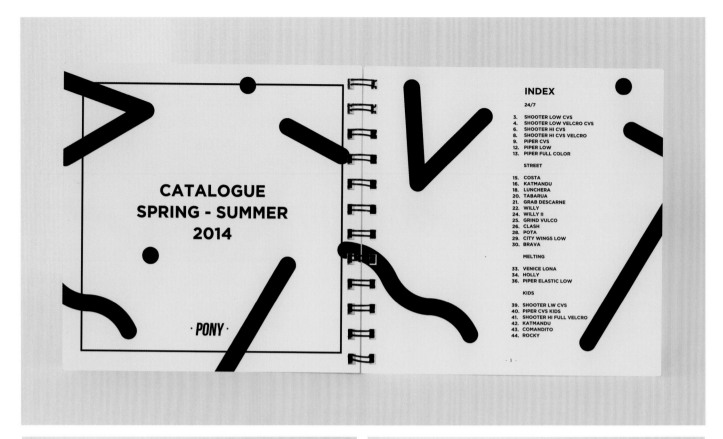

- 1 -

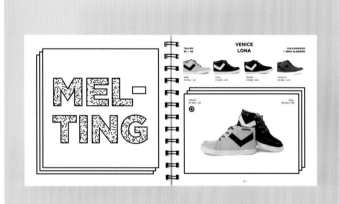

PONY SS 2014 Catalogue

Design Firm_Doradora Design Studio
Designer_Dolores Oliver
Client_PONY Argentina

This project is a spring-summer catalogue for PONY Argentina. It's a 48-page brochure, and is printed two-side in CMYK. The designer used yellow and black to form a strong visual impact. The designer also created pattern for the brochure, which was inspired by shoes. Additionally, random lines crawl on the page. All these elements combined make the whole design interesting and joyful.

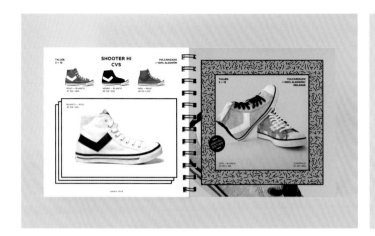

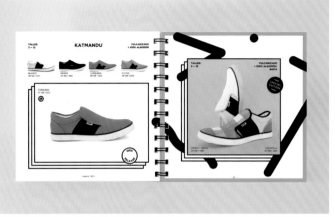

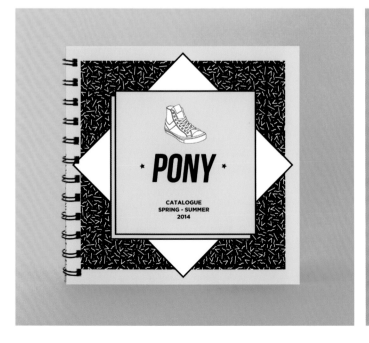

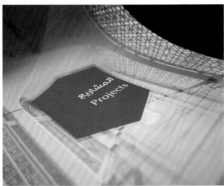

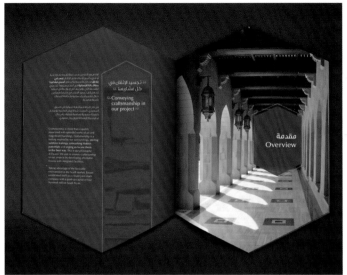

Ewaan Corporate Brochure

Designer_ Omar Reda
Photography_ Corbis
Client_ Ewaan

Ewaan is more than a company building real estate projects. It is dedicated to the craftsmanship involved with conceiving living communities that are inspired by people's surroundings. The brochure is based on their logo shape, and the layout is a perfect combination of aesthetic design and photos that are inspired by their core essence — craftsmanship.

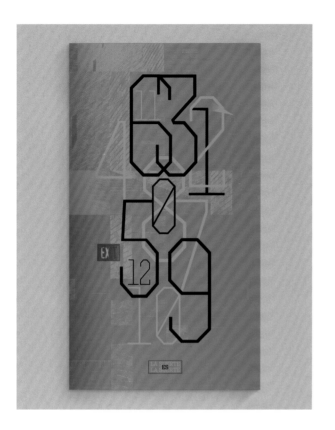

La suerte es la suerte

Designer_Federico Kanno
Client_Personal Work

La suerte es la suerte (luck is luck) is an editorial project based on *Cuentos para tahúres* (stories for tahures) by Rodolfo Walsh. After a complete analysis, the story was separated into parts and then linked with extra information about cops, gambling and guns, with the objective to expand and create a whole new version of the story. The analysis revealed the importance of numbers in the story, so it became the main approach. The numbers and their repetition, reinforced with overlaps, the image treatment and a solid grid give identity to the project.

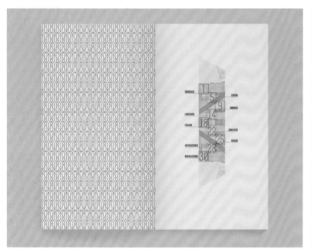

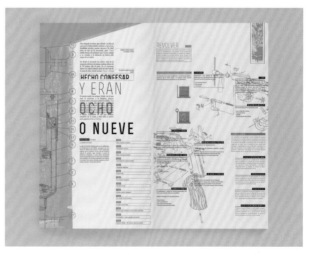

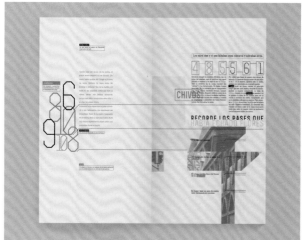

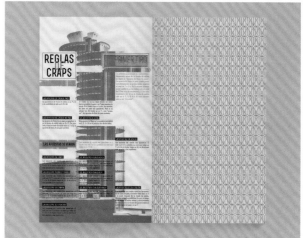

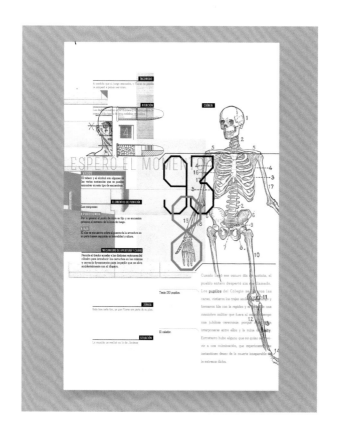

Stockholm City Guide

Design Firm_ Paloma Ernd/Design & Illustration
Designer_ Paloma Ernd
Photography_ Paloma Ernd
Client_ Personal Work

The design for this city guide is based on brown rustic paper mixed with bright orange color and raw black-and-white illustrations. It represents the city of Stockholm in its mixture of pristine nature and modern design attitude. The fold-out map is handy, with a Swedish sentence on the back which reads "Stockholm is a nice city": a fun way of showing the locals that readers may be interested in their language and a good first step to get in touch with them.

DON'T MISS THE EXPERIENCE
OF A SATURDAY MORNING
SHOPPING INCLUDING YOUR
COFFEE WITH SOME SWEDISH
PASTRY AFTER ALL.

A MOVIE AT AN INDEPENDENT
CINEMA, A RELAXING SUMMER
EVENING OR A TRIP THROUGH
THE BEST LIVE MUSIC CLUBS
IN SWEDEN.

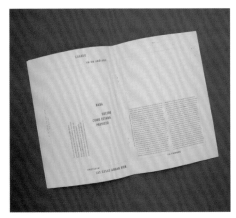

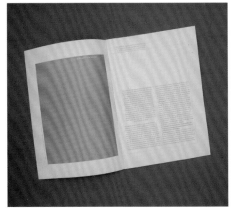

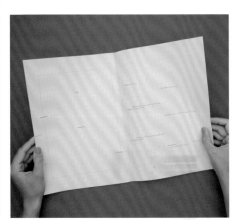

Vidas

Designer_Eugenia Mello
Photography_Eugenia Mello
Client_Personal Work

Vidas is an editorial project consisting of a serial system of fascicles, each containing a different interview of a well-known personality in Argentina. The design aims to dissect these deep, substantial and interesting conversations. Hidden messages, different voices, and tones were applied in the design. Through a typographic approach, the pages translated the varied overlapping layers, tones and colors of the interviews into lively visuals.

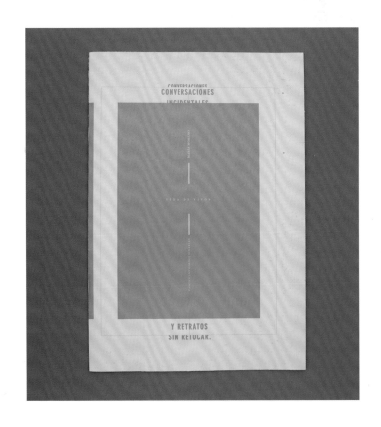

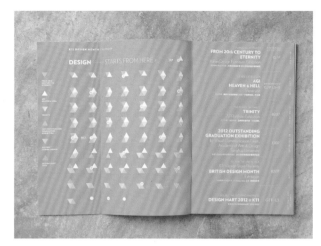

K11 Design Month

Design Firm_JKwan Design
Photography_Jason Kwan
Client_K11 Concepts

K11, located in Hong Kong, is claimed to be the world's first art mall. JKwan Design designed the logotype and promotional booklet for last year's K11 Design Month with the mall's art team. The logotype exhibits a vibrant combination of font styles, resulting in a distinctive look with a hair-thin line subtly connecting the letter, which aptly echoes with K11's consistent goal of linking dynamic artists and designers with the mass audience. The brochure includes a well-organized event calendar, followed with a detailed introduction of the event, and features interviews of notable artists and designers, which were well laid out to present a comprehensive picture.

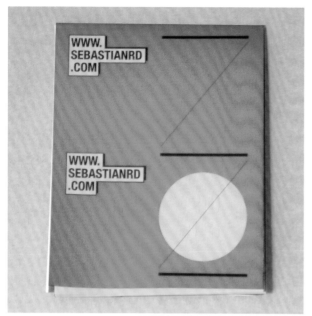

Self Promotion

Design Firm_ Sebastián Ruiz Díaz Design
Photography_ Sebastián Ruiz Díaz
Client_ Personal Work

For 2013, the designer decided to make a self-promotion booklet of his work for his current and future customers, giving an explanation of what is design as applied in different fields of communication. The piece is divided into different sections: editorial, branding, posters, and other design areas. The result is this mini brochure in which the newest designs are displayed in a creative way: bright colors, bold design of the text and skillful overlays, all of which contribute to an amazing layout.

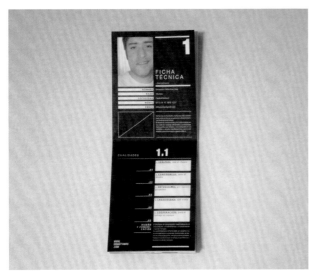

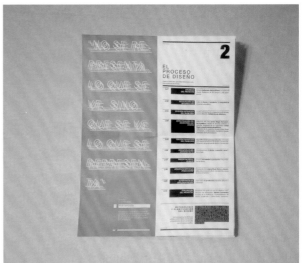

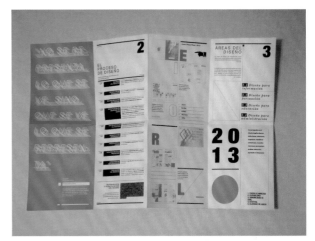

The Sign

Designer_Wildan Ilham
Photography_Livina Intania
Client_Personal Work

This was a school project made in a typography class. The goal was to make this newsletter become more explorative. The designer used many geometric shapes, duotone colors and many fonts to create a newsletter with a unique style.

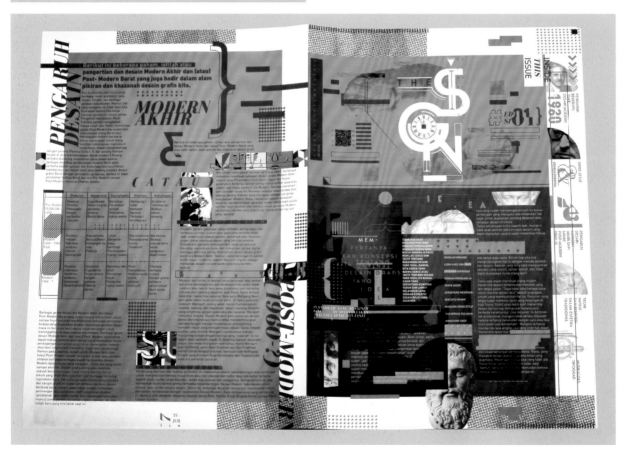

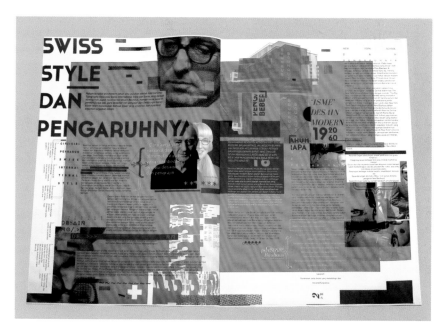

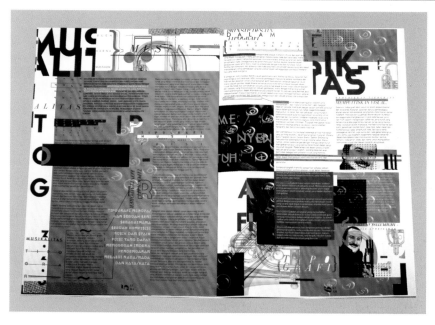

Circular Supplement
— A Typographic Guide

Designer_Joshua Elliff
Photography_Joshua Elliff
Client_D&AD

This is a supplement designed to introduce to readers the designers and directors speaking at The Typographic Circle events. The designer loosely used the idea of a timeline; he included bios and interviews. All are presented in a multi-format booklet to give the viewer multiple interactions.

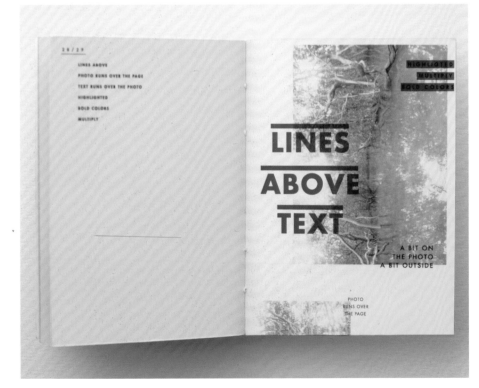

Easy Design

Designer_Beste Birer
Photography_Vincent Schwenk
Client_Personal Work

This sarcastic pocket guide shows both basic and trendy elements in random combinations. People can use any element in different combinations to achieve (relatively) different results. In the layout, images and texts are arranged leisurely; nonetheless, the whole design is concise and informative.

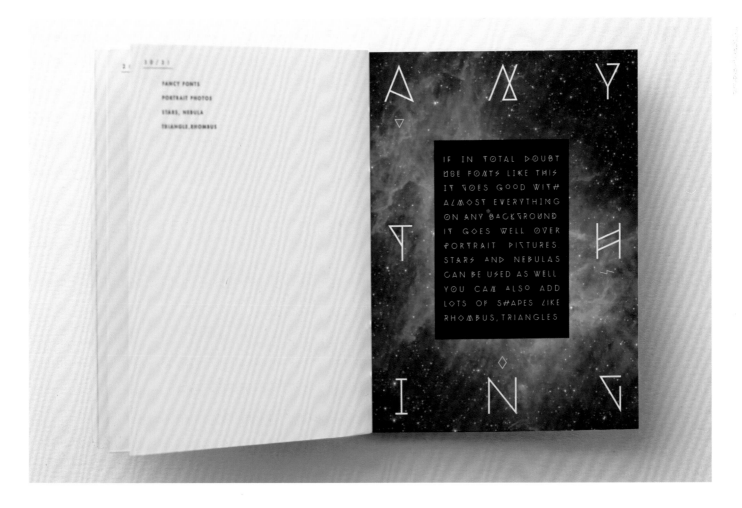

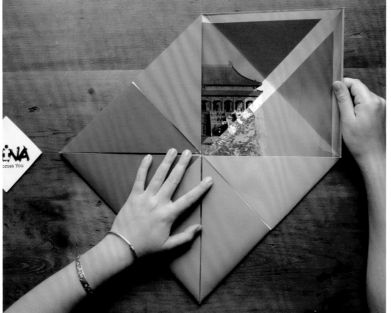

Branding China

Designer_Ivy Zheyu Chen
Photography_Ivy Zheyu Chen
Client_Personal Work

In this imaginary branding project for China tourism, the designer separated China into four regions: North, East, South, and West. She chose a color to represent each region and lead readers to know its distinctive sceneries, people and culture. Four brochures are integrated into a systematic encyclopedia of China.

Kunst ist, wenn Beethoven singt

Design Firm_Rasmus und christin
Photography_Rasmus und christin
Client_Sabine Feldwieser, Die Wortfinder e.V

This fictitious book performs as a two-dimensional stage for art and *belles lettres* made by people with an intellectual disability. The texts were created in the creative workshops by Sabine Feldwieser, Die Wortfinder e.V. The book consists of four chapters in different sizes and shows art and texts, which are inspired by each other. These four parts of the book reflect and demonstrate the work and progress of the creative workshop.

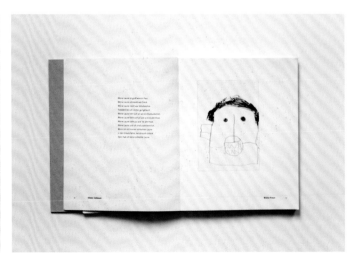

POSTER

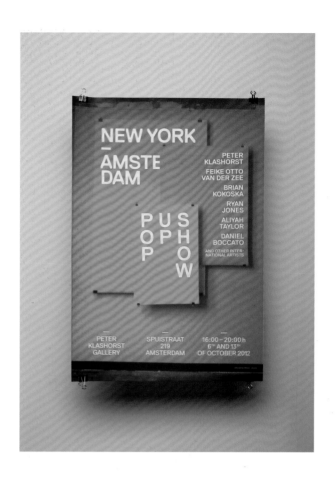

New York–Amsterdam Pop-up Show

Design Firm_OK200
Client_Peter Klashorst Gallery

OK200 designed and silkscreen printed the posters and flyers for an exhibition for artists from Amsterdam and New York. They've created sixteen unique flyers by using one of the background layers out of the poster and printing the flyer information on top.

L'Auditori de Barcelona

Design Firm_Toormix
Photography_Toormix
Client_L'Auditori de Barcelona

This set of posters formed a part of a new campaign for the Auditori de Barcelona. Innovative graphics become the upper structure of the building; the creative concept is based on the idea of the building as a Jack-in-the-box.

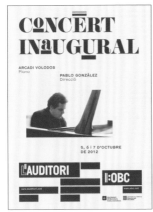

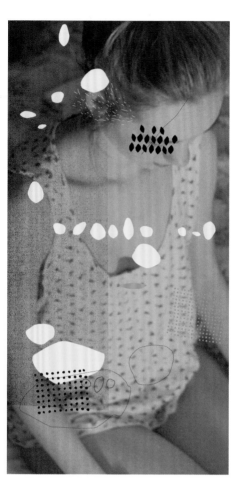

LA I Festival de vocalistas femeninas

Design Firm_Doradora Design Studio
Designer_Dolores Oliver
Client_Personal Work

LA was created for a fictional female vocalist's festival. The concept was using the artist's voice as promotional elements. It shows youth, freshness, dynamism, and a feel of sensitivity. The designer tried to find graphic resources that show the spirit of the festival as something friendly and fresh. She chose a soft palette, analog photographs and female objects including a teapot, flowers, rollers, and other objects. Most of its typography was hand-drawn to show sensitivity and informality.

LA I Festival de vocalistas femeninas — Special Show

Design Firm_Doradora Design Studio
Designer_Dolores Oliver
Client_Personal Work

This graphic identity was made for the special show of M.I.A. (an English Sri Lankan recording artist), which will take place during LA Festival. This project includes different graphic pieces: two colorful, gold-coated posters, a 24-page press book with detailed information about the artist, and a souvenir that includes a surprise kit for hair dye which would be delivered by hand. The overall design is full of lively atmosphere and creates visual enjoyment for the viewers.

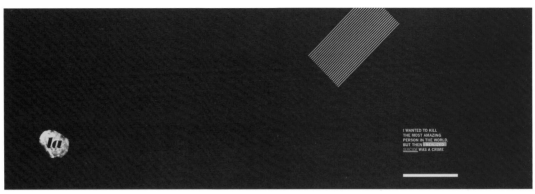

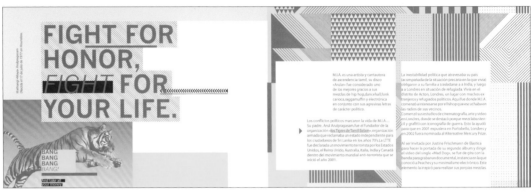

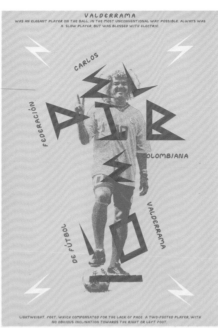

VALDERRAMA
WAS AN ELEGANT PLAYER ON THE BALL. IN THE MOST UNCONVENTIONAL WAY POSSIBLE. ALWAYS WAS
A SLOW PLAYER, BUT WAS BLESSED WITH ELECTRIC.

CARLOS

FEDERACIÓN

COLOMBIANA

VALDERRAMA

DE FÚTBOL

LIGHTWEIGHT, FEET, WHICH COMPENSATED FOR THE LACK OF PACE. A TWO-FOOTED PLAYER, WITH
NO OBVIOUS INCLINATION TOWARDS THE RIGHT OR LEFT FOOT.

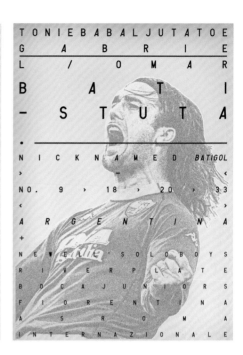

TONIEBABALJUTATOE
GABRIE
L/OMAR
BATI
-STUTA
•
NICKNAMED BATIGOL
NO. 9 › 18 › 20 › 33
ARGENTINA
NEWELL'SOLDBOYS
RIVERPLATE
BOCAJUNIORS
FIORENTINA
ASROMA
INTERNAZIONALE

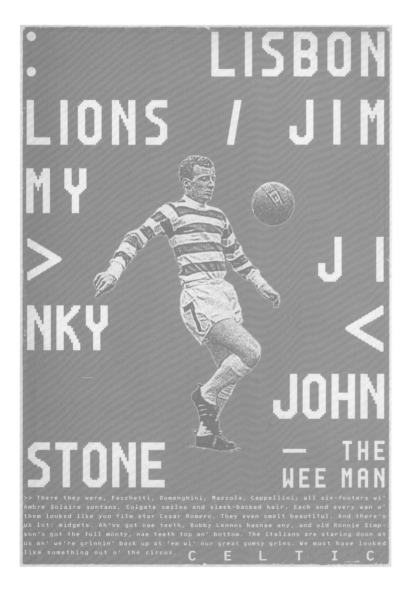

LISBON
LIONS / JIM
MY
> JI
NKY <
JOHN
STONE — THE
WEE MAN

>> There they were, Facchetti, Domenghini, Mazzola, Cappellini; all six-footers wi'
Ambre Solaire suntans, Colgate smiles and sleek-backed hair. Each and every wan o'
them looked like yon film star Cesar Romero. They even smelt beautiful. And there's
us lot: midgets. Ah've got nae teeth, Bobby Lennox hasnae any, and old Ronnie Simp-
son's got the full monty, nae teeth top an' bottom. The Italians are staring doon at
us an' we're grinnin' back up at 'em wi' our great gumsy grins. We must have looked
like something out o' the circus. C E L T I C

Sucker for Soccer

Designer_Zoran Lucić
Client_Personal Work

This self-initiated poster series was made to put football into new perspectives. For the designer, the game is extremely inspiring as a social event as well as a sporting phenomenon, and it deserves much more than the one-dimensional treatment that has been used before. By putting artwork into retro aesthetics, the designer attempts to combine the last fifty years of the game into one unique graphic language.

GoGo Penguin Tour

Designer_Daniel Reed
Client_GoGo Penguin + Roller Trio

This is a poster series for GoGo Penguin + Roller Trio's UK tour. The designs were inspired by the band's strong musical melodies and vocals, and their ability to keep perfect timing when playing complex riffs. The illustration in black is a representation of piano keys, as each band uses the piano as the main source of melody within the trios.

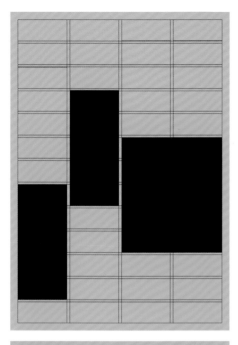

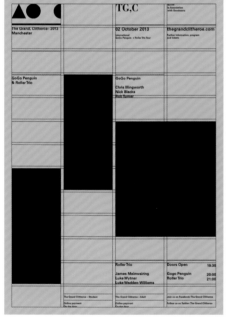

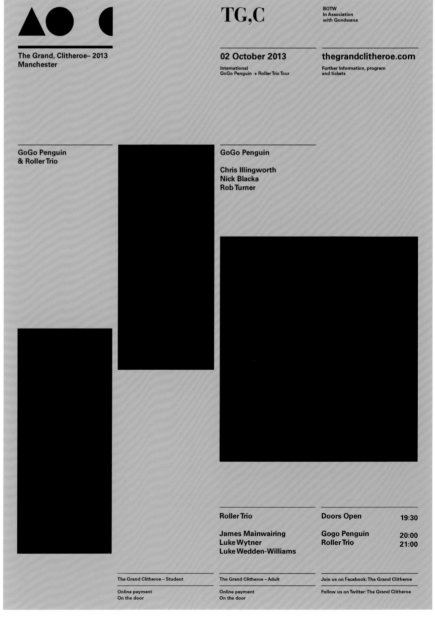

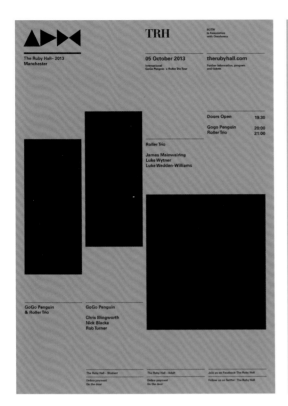

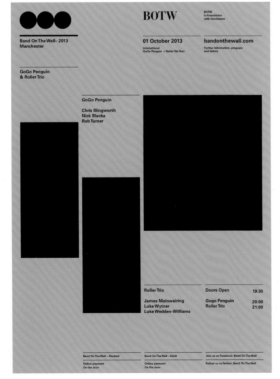

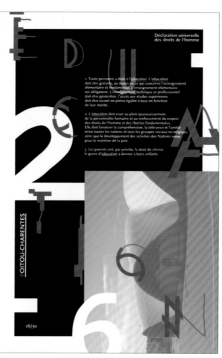

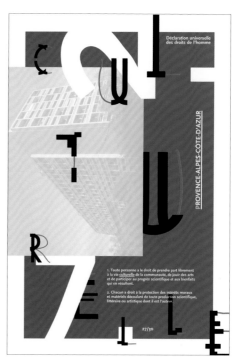

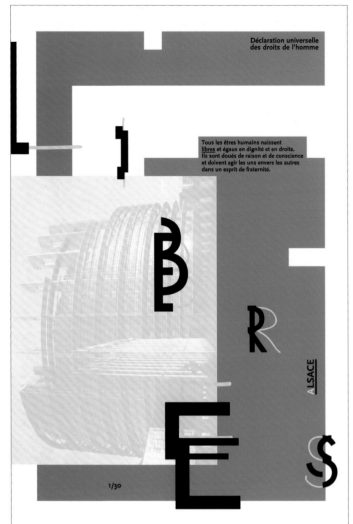

1Point

Designer_Alexandre Tonneau
Photography_Alexandre Tonneau
Client_Personal Work

1 Point is a project about the Universal Declaration of Human Rights (1948). The ambition of this project is to introduce into the current national debate the issues, topics and values of the Universal Declaration of Human Rights, which are developed through the preamble and the thirty-one articles. The project is composed of thirty-one posters, thirty-one flyers, a book and a website (www.1point.fr). The designer created a new typeface and combined it with colorful backgrounds, which creates visual enjoyment for the viewers.

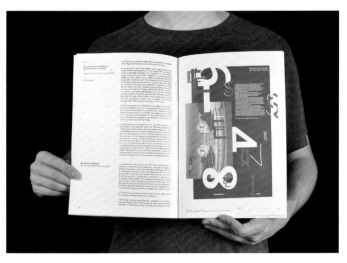

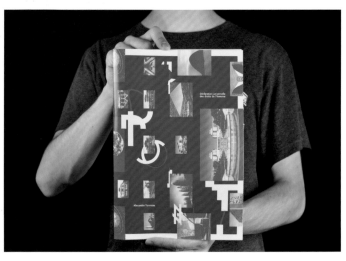

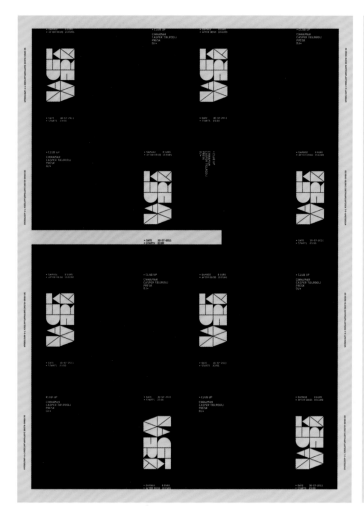

Nachtwerk

Design Firm_HOAX
Photography_HOAX
Client_Nachtwerk

Nachtwerk (Nightwork) is a nightclub in Amsterdam focused
on modern bass music. As a brand-consultant, HOAX created
an identity and poster-series for Nachtwerk. Frugally minded,
the design firm created a poster which could be cut up into
eight flyers — each with a different front — resulting in an
abstract but recognizable identity. Every new poster is printed
on a lighter color paper than the previous one, representing a
sunrise.

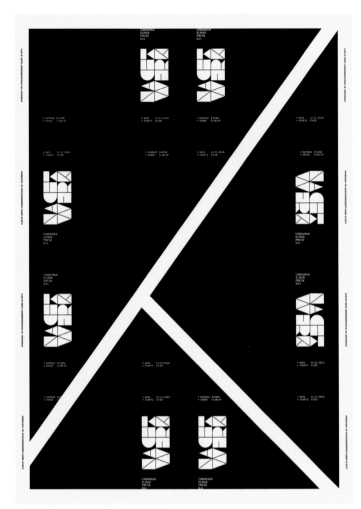

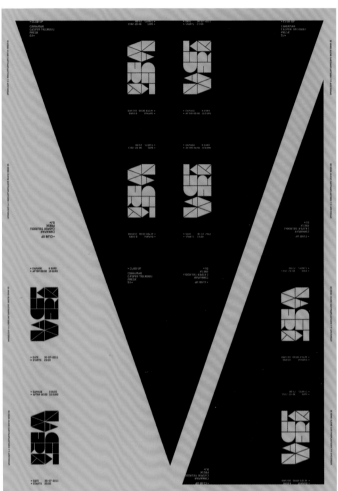

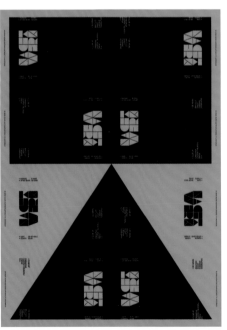

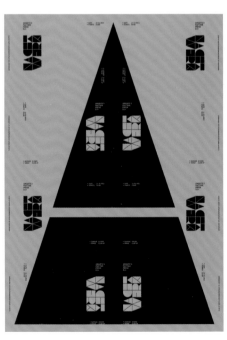

Designeyland

Design Firm_ Rational International
Designer_ Ivorin Vrkaš
Photography_ Ivorin Vrkaš
Client_ Coworking Croatia

Designeyland is an ironic play on the mish-mash of various events and activities that calls upon associations with Disneyland — the crown jewel of activity-packed places. The digital visuals were created for all the immediate and necessary online communications. For the posters, many bright colors were chosen to form a distinctive visual impact; overlaid irregular figures look complicated and kaleidoscopic. The whole design shows people a free and fancy world.

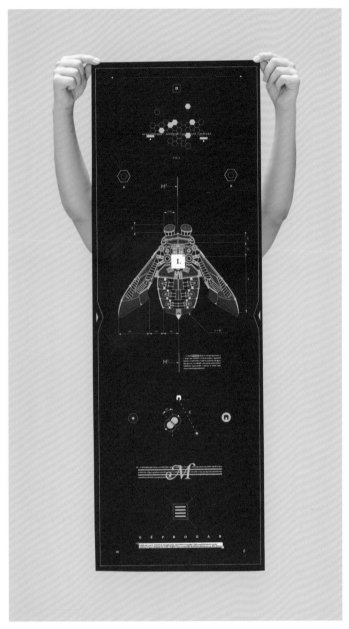

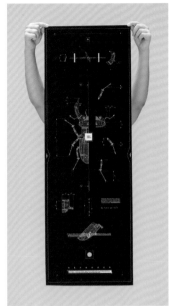

Mechanical Insects

Designer_Marton Borzak
Photography_Marton Borzak
Client_Personal Work

This is a self-initiated project of the designer and was sent out to clients as a gift. Every design has its own blueprint, accompanied by textual and visual information about the chosen insect. Interesting facts were visualized and shown with personal opinions about the specific insect. It was produced with great care in a limited run.

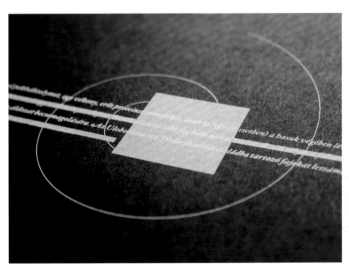

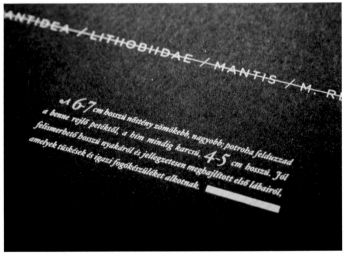

Republique

Design Firm_Scandinavian DesignLab
Creative Director_Per Madsen
Designers_Per Madsen, Robert Daniel Nagy
Photography_Scandinavian DesignLab
Client_Republique Theatre

This project was created for the new Danish theatre based in Copenhagen called Republique. A decision was made to create a series of image posters that promote the individual performance at the theatre. The circle symbolizes a community of shared values across nationality, gender and age and serves as a reminder that you — the audience — is at the center of all that Republique does.

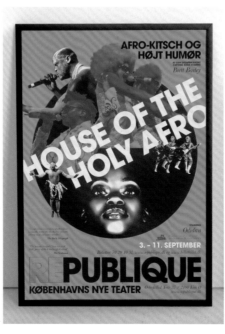

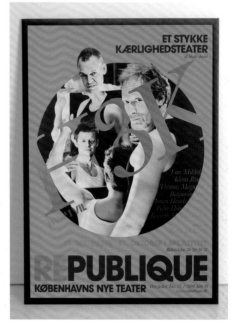

OTHERS

Mikser Festival 2012

Design Firm_Lorem Ipsum Studio
Creative Directors_Nemanja Jehlicka, Bratislav Milenkovic, Nikola Zmajevic
Photography_Milica Mrvic
Client_Mikser

The concept for this project was based on the change of the festival's location, from Žitomlin to Savamala. Designers wanted to create the feeling of movement and dispersion to reflect the festival's new location and its program. The result is dynamic fonts spreading throughout all print materials. The contrast between black and yellow forms a strong visual impact.

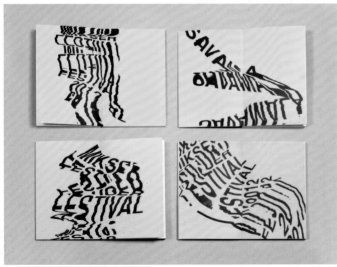

FAMU Student Film Festival 2011 — Weightlessness

Design Firm_Kolektiv Studio
Designers_Lukáš Kijonka, Michal Krůl
Photography_Michal Krůl
Client_FAMU Prague

Weightlessness is a visual identity created for FAMU Student Film Festival and party, including the alphabetical sorting system of information and following applications (posters and brochures). Designers chose yellow as the main color, which contrasts with the black letters, to create a refreshing feeling. There are also yellow elements on each page, the style of which maintains consistency with the cover.

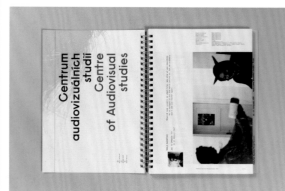

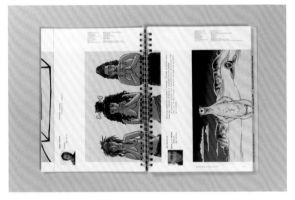

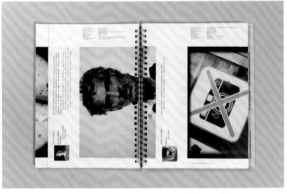

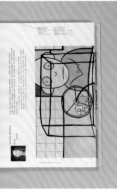

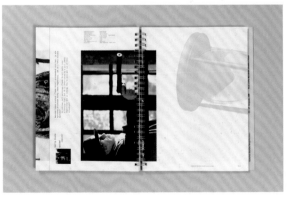

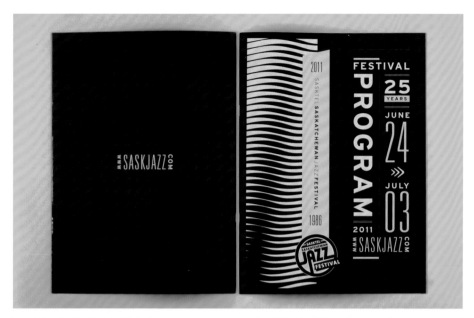

Saskatchewan Jazz Festival

Design Firm_Firebelly Design
Designers_Will Miller, Darren McPherson, Nick Adam, Colin White
Client_Saskatchewan Jazz Festival

For Saskatchewan Jazz Festival's 25th anniversary, Firebelly reinvented and redesigned its visual identity. Typographically, dynamic blocks of bold and informative text framed and shaped the pages of each piece, allowing the juxtaposition of type and image to move the viewer's eye in both rhythmic and spontaneous ways. A bold pattern representing vibration, used in different ways throughout the series of pieces, was established as an anchor to the Festival's location and a subtle reference to musical reverberation.

Beirut Revival

Designer_Hiba Jaroudi
Client_Hj Designs

Beirut Revival is an abundance of inspiring work focused on restructuring the collective memory of people through visual themes. Designed on canvas, the layers of each work tell a charming story. Hiba's concept is to feature, through various media, the city's dynamics and its people. She elegantly visualized grand moments from the past and related them to our daily life of the present. Be it a photo, a text, newspaper clippings, or calligraphy, the work narrates beautifully a happy story that happened somewhere, witnessing the uniqueness of a place she calls home.

DESIGNED BY HIBA JAROUDI

Clothing
Fashions

Early Western travelers, whether to Persia, Turkey absence of changes in fashion there, and observers on the unseemly pace of Western fashion, which m lack of order in Western culture. The Japanese Shogly accurately) to a Spanish visitor in 1609 that Jap over a thousand years.[2] However in Ming China, evidence for rapidly changing fashions in Chinese often took place at times of economic or social cha the medieval Caliphate); but then a long period wit occurred in Moorish Spain from the 8th century, wi introduced sophisticated clothing styles based on n native Baghdad and his own inspiration to Córdoba changes in fashion occurred in the Middle East fro arrival of the Turks, who introduced clothing styles The beginnings of the habit in Europe of continual clothing styles can be fairly reliably dated to the m historians including James Laver and Fernand Bra in clothing.[7][8] The most dramatic manifestation tightening of the male over-garment, from calf-len sometimes accompanied with stuffing on the chest

Early Western travelers, whether to Persia, Turkey absence of changes in fashion there, and observers on the unseemly pace of Western fashion, which m lack of order in Western culture. The Japanese Shogly accurately) to a Spanish visitor in 1609 that Jap over a thousand years.[2] However in Ming China, evidence for rapidly changing fashions in Chinese often took place at times of economic or social cha the medieval Caliphate); but then a long period wit occurred in Moorish Spain from the 8th century, wi introduced sophisticated clothing styles based on n native Baghdad and his own inspiration to Córdoba changes in fashion occurred in the Middle East fro arrival of the Turks, who introduced clothing styles The beginnings of the habit in Europe of continual clothing styles can be fairly reliably dated to the m historians including James Laver and Fernand Bra in clothing.[7][8] The most dramatic manifestation tightening of the male over-garment, from calf-len distinctive Western male outline of a tailored top w

Jeans
Starting in the 1950s
Denim trousers for sailors

ns (at the time known as "dungarees"), along with ligh soiled "cambric" shirts, became part of the official wo orm of the United States Navy in the first part of the tury. A working uniform was selected to protect track storms from becoming soiled or torn in the ship's rug king environment, leaving them for ceremonial occas ey were first issued in 1901, and were originally sho t but by the mid 20th century the trousers became th e to permit ventilation in the ship's hotter working en its and to ensure sailors could shed their dungarees i felt overboard or had to abandon ship. ame type of uniform consisting of jeans and chambr used as prison uniforms in some correctional facilitie sue of the durability and low-maintenance of denim deemed suitable for the rugged manual labor carrie nmates. A popular example of the use of denim as p wear can be seen in the film Cool Hand Luke

ns (at the time known as "dungarees"), along with ligh soiled "cambric" shirts, became part of the official wo orm of the United States Navy in the first part of the tury. A working uniform was selected to protect track storms from becoming soiled or torn in the ship's rug king environment, leaving them for ceremonial occas ey were first issued in 1901, and were originally sho t but by the mid 20th century the trousers became th e to permit ventilation in the ship's hotter working en its and to ensure sailors could shed their dungarees i felt overboard or had to abandon ship. ame type of uniform consisting of jeans and chambr used as prison uniforms in some correctional facilitie sue of the durability and low-maintenance of denim deemed suitable for the rugged manual labor carrie nmates. A popular example of the use of denim as p wear can be seen in the film Cool Hand Luke

Peach
Species of Prunus

Bread
Popular around the world
& the world's oldest foods

Fresh bread is prized for its taste, aroma, quality, appearance and texture

Bread is one of the oldest prepared foods

Cultural & political importance of bread

Bread is one of the oldest prepared foods. Evidence from 30,000 years ago in Europe revealed starch residue on rocks used for pounding plants.[2] It is possible that during this time, starch extrac from the roots of plants, such as cattails and ferns, was spread on a flat rock, placed over a fire and cooked into a primitive form of flatbread. Around 10,000 BC, with the dawn of the Neolithic age and the spread of agriculture, grains became the mainstay of makin bread. Yeast spores are ubiquitous, including the surface of cereal grains, so any dough left to rest will become naturally leavened. There were multiple sources of leavening available for early bread Antoine steaks could be harnessed by leaving uncooked dough exposed to air for some time before cooking. Pliny the Elder reporte that the Gauls and Iberians used the foam skimmed from beer to produce "a lighter kind of bread than other peoples." Parts of the ancient world that drank wine instead of beer used a paste compos of grape juice and flour that was allowed to begin fermenting, or wh bran steeped in wine, as a source for yeast. The most common sou of leavening was to retain a piece of dough from the previous day t use as a form of sourdough starter.

Bread is one of the oldest prepared foods. years ago in Europe revealed starch resi pounding plants.[2] It is possible that dur from the roots of plants, such as cattails on a flat rock, placed over a fire and coo of flatbread. Around 10,000 BC, with the and the spread of agriculture, grains bec bread. Yeast spores are ubiquitous, inclu grains, so any dough left to rest will beco There were multiple sources of leavening Antoine steaks could be harnessed by lea exposed to air for some time before cook that the Gauls and Iberians used the foam produce "a lighter kind of bread than other ancient world that drank wine instead of of grape juice and flour that was allowed bran steeped in wine, as a source for yea of leavening was to retain a piece of doug use as a form of sourdough starter.

A major advance happened in 1961 with the development of the Chorleywood bread process, which used the intense mechanical working of dough to dramatically reduce the fermentation period an the time taken to produce a loaf. The process, whose high-energy mixing allows for the use of lower protein grain, is now widely used around the world in large factories.

Recently, domestic bread machines which automate the process of making bread have become popular.

Keyline SpA Rebranding

Design Firm_ Massimo Künstler
Designers_ Massimo Künstler, Andrea Dell'Anna, Francesco D'Urso
Client_ Keyline SpA

Keyline SpA is an innovative, market-leading Italian company operating worldwide in the field of design and production of keys and key cutting machines. In this massive project, the designers took care of the company's total rebranding, from new logo design to corporate guideline manual, product brochures, packaging, trade show stands, websites system, merchandising, institutional communication, and all other methods of communication. Designers chose red and black to form a strong contrast. The layout is dynamic, flexible, and catches readers' eyes at first sight glance.

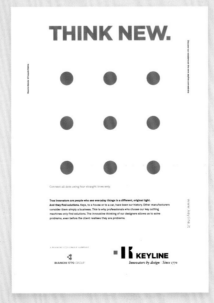

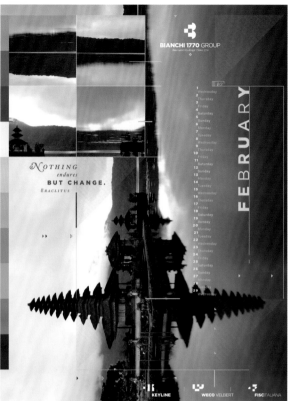

Bianchi 1770 Group — Calendar 2012

Design Firm_Massimo Künstler
Designers_Massimo Künstler, Andrea Dell'Anna, Francesco D'Urso
Client_Bianchi 1770 Group

Bianchi 1770 Group operates in the competitive field of design and production for security experts (such as automotive transponder key technology, key cutting machines, mechanization applied to furnishings and plastic components). The designers created a new identity for the group. Here is their 2012 calendar, where lines and points are properly applied. The result is an amazing layout which is modern and free.

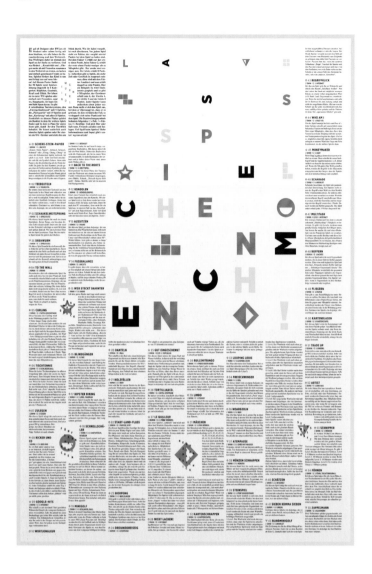

WG Turnier

Designer_Vincent Schwenk
Photography_Vincent Schwenk
Client_Personal Work

When the designer was living in a WG (shared living community), he was thinking of finding a funny way to spend some "offline" time with his roommates, so he developed a modern game collection with fifty-five games in four different categories. He also designed a main poster and an additional magazine for more games. In the layout, Tetris figures and letters were arranged in an interesting way, highlighting the fun of the games; moreover, they make the design more vivid.

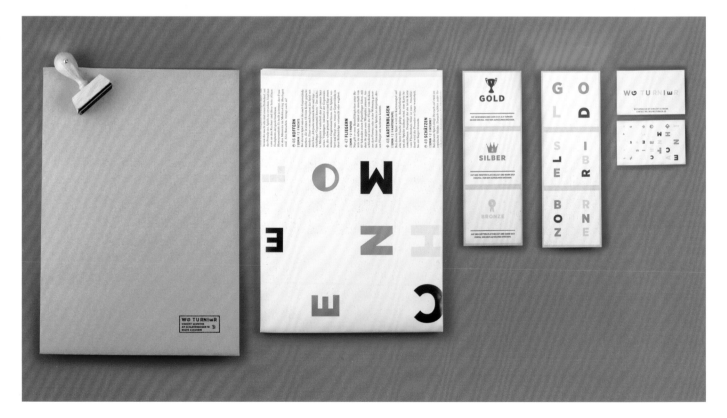

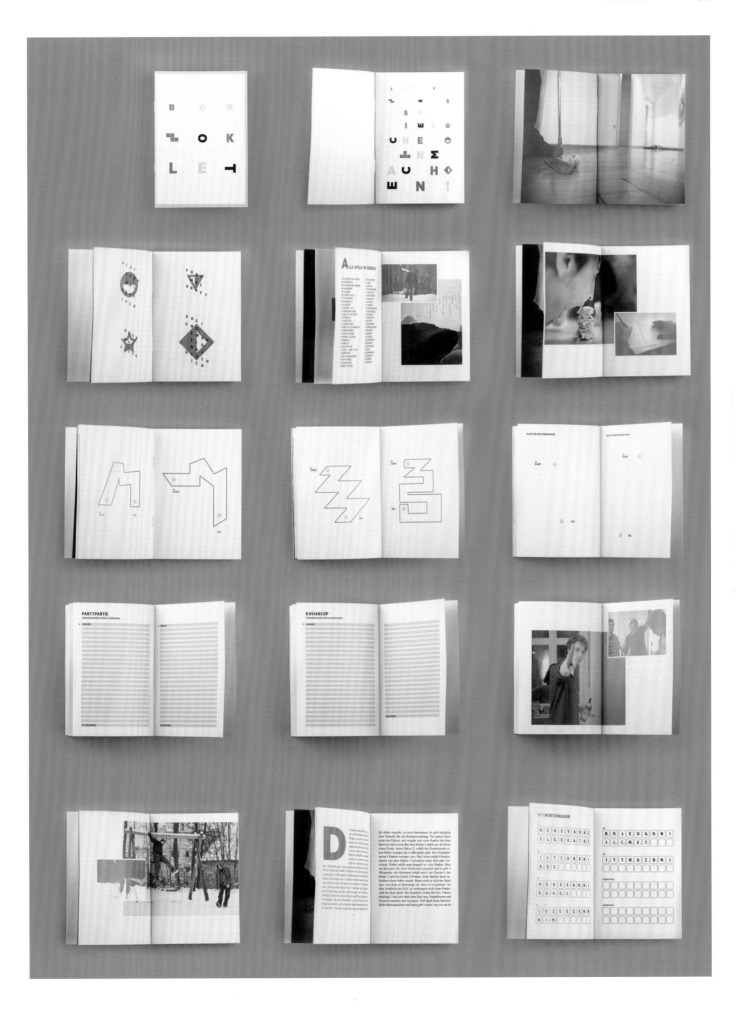

Symphonesia Rebranding

Designer_Hadid Windoro
Client_Student's Senate of International Relations Department, Padjadjaran University

This project was created for an annual multi-event, "Symphonesia," organized by the students of Padjadjaran University's Department of International Relations. This year, it focuses on diversity issues in both national and international realms, using "Anthem of Diversity" as its official theme. For its print materials, the designer chose bright colors, which are associated with fun. The firm lines show that Symphonesia is an event that has a strong structure inside. Lines were connected to each other describing an interconnectivity that became the main weapon of value dissemination of international relations.

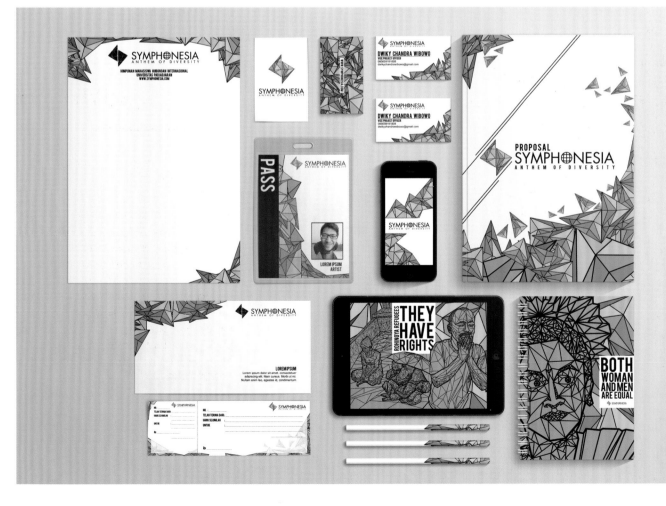

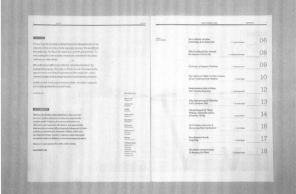

99U Conference Branding 2013

Creative Director_Matias Corea
Designers_Raewyn Brandon, Matias Corea
Photography_Raewyn Brandon
Client_The 99U Conference

The approach for the 2013 99U Conference materials embodied a light, bright feeling as the designers played with a bold fluorescent color (Pantone 805 U) on white backgrounds, with periodic accents of black. To push the language of the 99U brand forward, Hoefler & Frere-Jone's serif font Sentinel was chosen. Designers focused heavily on typography and used the beautiful letterforms as large shapes, then added delicate, detailed patterns to give depth to the designs.

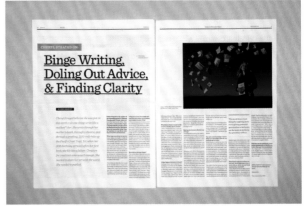

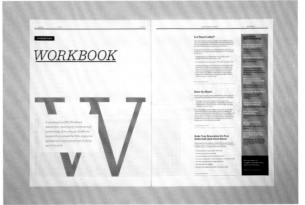
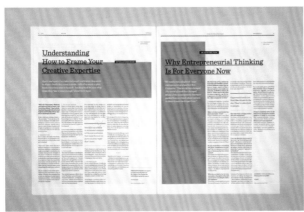

238

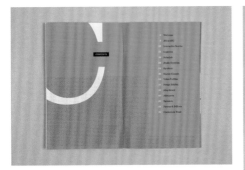

Punchers Plant

Design Firm_Paloma Ernd I Design & Illustration
Designer_Paloma Ernd
Photography_Punchers Plant
Client_Punchers Plant

The band Punchers Plant wanted a special booklet for their record "How to Escape." Since their budget was small, the production was planned as a DIY project. The printed sheets were hand-cut, bound by using a sewing machine, and stamped by hand. The design was reduced to black and white; the red yarn is referring to the key visual element of the artwork, a red eye. For promotional purposes, artwork posters doubled as dust jackets for the booklets.

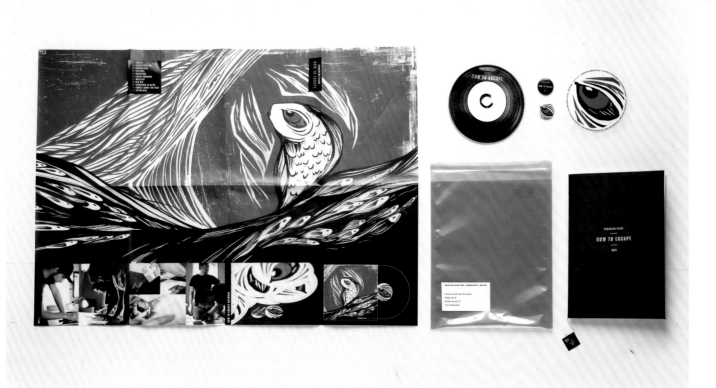

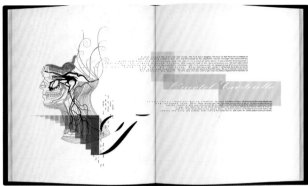

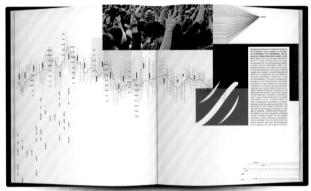

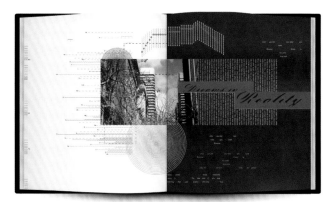

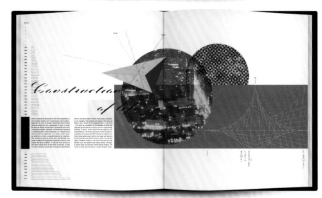

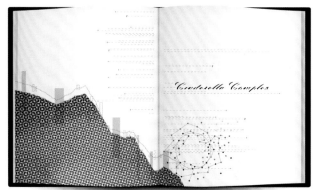

Cinderella Complex

Designer_ Ju Lee
Photography_ Ju Lee
Client_ Personal Work

This is a paper line promotion project in the forms of a book and a website presenting the designer's own message. More specifically, it is telling a visual story of how things that are possible in a fantasy are hard or impossible to get in real life. The project consists of fantasy vs. reality elements, and visual elements that bridge the differences between fantasy and reality. Welcome to an unconventional and experimental world!

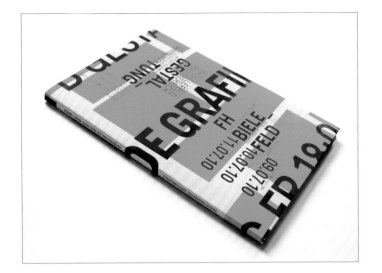

Diplomkatalog

Designers_Christin Ferri, Johannes Nathow, Christian Andreas, Alex Katchko, Maria Arndt, Clarissa Becker
Photography_Christin Ferri
Client_Personal Work

This catalogue came with the exhibition of the final design exams at the University of Applied Sciences in Bielefeld, Germany. The catalogue shows an overview of all the graduates and their projects for the year. The concept was to visualize the problem of multitasking, so designers overlaid pictures and texts to make it difficult to read and assign the projects. The poster for the exhibition was printed on different paper, cut to different sizes and used as posters, flyers, and covers for the catalogues.

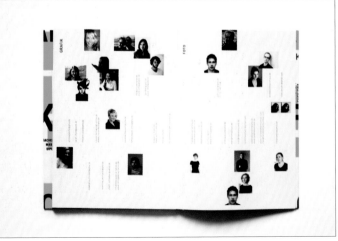

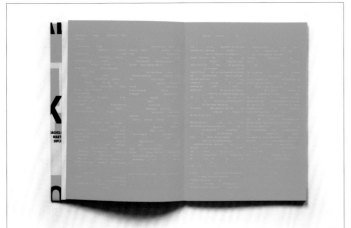

Humanized Platform

Designer_Ju Lee
Photography_Ju Lee
Client_Personal Work

In the attempt to combine human emotions and computer technology, the designer pays a nostalgic tribute to the social communications among the designers before computer technology dominated the world. They wrote letters, met each other to share their actual emotions, be it positive or not. By creating a new art form, this work aims to make the modern life more personal.

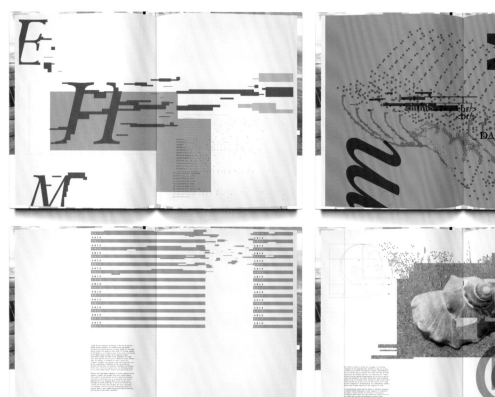

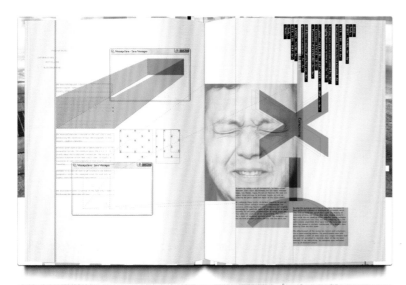

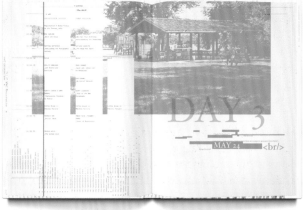

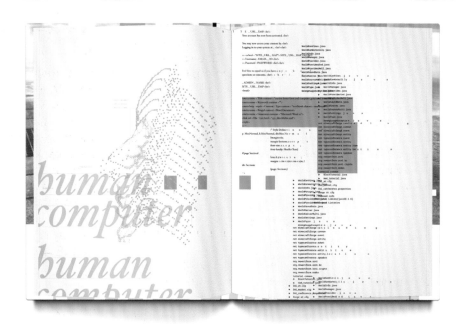

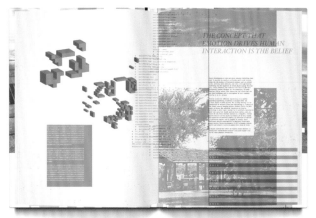

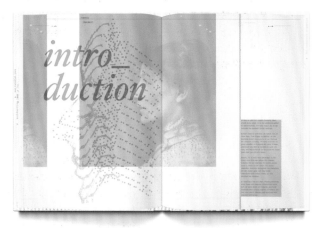

INDEX

Alain Vonck

Location: Paris, France
Tel: 06 51 58 6289
Web: www.alainvonck.com

Alain Vonck is a young graphic designer from Paris. He began his design studio in 2012 after graduating with the highest honors from ESAG Penninghen School in Paris. Since then, he has worked for various commercial clients in France. He has also developed an artistic practice around Internet art and that media's new aesthetic.

Alexandre Tonneau

Location: Paris, France
Email: contact@alexandretonneau.fr
Web: www.alexandretonneau.fr

Alexandre Tonneau is a French freelance graphic designer with a Bachelor of Art in Graphic Design from the Institut supérieur des arts appliqués (Lisaa Paris), based in Paris. He develops his graphic design practice in print and digital fields, creating editorial design, visual identity, web design, motion design, iPhone and iPad apps.

Alice Rinaudo

Location: Torino, Italy
Email: alice.rinaudo@deltatre.com
Web: www.behance.net/Aly: rinaudo

Alice Rinaudo was born in Torino in 1990. She attended a classical high school and now holds a Doctorate in Graphic Design from Polytechnic of Turin. During university studies, she worked for the UXD design section in a media company in Torino called "Deltatre." Nowadays she lives in Milano, pursuing a master degree in Visual Brand Design at Domus Academy.

Angelica Baini

Location: Miami, USA
Email: angelica.baini@gmail.com
Web: angelicabaini.com

Angelica Baini is a multi-disciplinary designer, born in the town of Castiglion Fiorentino, Italy, on January 28, 1990. She is a recent graduate who double majored in Graphic Design and Digital Media at New World School of the Arts in Miami, Florida.

Another Day

Location: Nijmegen, Netherlands
Tel: +31 06 835 614 67
Web: www.studioanotherday.nl

Another Day is the graphic design studio of Yorick de Vries. Yorick was born in 1985 in Lelystad, the Netherlands. Now he lives and works in Nijmegen. In 2012, Yorick started the studio "Another Day." Another Day's main focus lies in the field of art and culture with a specialization on typography and printed matter.

Atelier d'alves

Location: Porto, Portugal
Tel: +351 222 086 867
Web: www.atelierdalves.com

Atelier d'alves is the natural culmination of a path trodden with enthusiasm since 2009, when Sergio Alves began working independently with clients from a range of areas. His diverse experience was essential for the creation and consolidation of a personal philosophy and form. The work of the studio responds to the needs of emerging visual communication in all areas, especially in the field of culture — theatre, architecture, dance and literature.

BachGärde

Location: Stockholm, Sweden
Tel: +46 70 518 22 91
Web: www.bachgarde.com

BachGärde is a design agency founded in 2007 by graphic designer Marcus Gärde and designer Linnéa Bach Gärde. Marcus started working in graphic design in 2002 after graduating from Forsbergs School of Advertising in Stockholm, Sweden. Two years later he started giving lectures and seminars in typography and is at present Course Administrator in Typography at the three major design schools in Stockholm. Marcus is also the author of three books; *Typografins Väg*, *Typografins väg II* and *Megalithic Temples of Malta*.

Benoît Bodhuin

Location: Lille, France
Email: bb@bb-bureau.fr
Web: www.bb-bureau.fr

After studying mathematics at university, enrolling at a school of graphic design, and a short stint in some agencies, Benoît Bodhuin exercises now this profession as an independent graphic designer in Lille, France. He works freely in alternating personal projects and orders from clients with a consciousness about their images, mainly focusing on graphic identity, publishing, typography, and web design.

Beste Birer

Location: Graz, Austria
Tel: +43 681 81791069
Web: www.bestebirer.com

Beste Birer was born and raised in Turkey, and graduated from the Graphic Design Department of Mimar Sinan Fine Arts University in Istanbul. She currently lives in Austria, working at moodley brand identity.

Boris Vargas Vasquez

Location: Buenos Aires, Argentina
Tel: +54 9(11)34760905
Web: www.behance.net/BorisVargas

Boris Vargas Vasquez is a graphic designer from Argentina. Born in 1990, Boris graduated from the University of Buenos Aires. Constantly looking for inspiration, some years ago he found his love for typography, and has always been passionate about everything visual and artistic. He is fond of the universe, highly detailed work, and clearly structured designs. Boris has served for international agencies and editorials such as JODI studio of Brooklyn, NY, The 420 Times of California, and the David Bitton Group of Miami, FL.

Brian Banton

Location: Toronto, Canada
Email: brian@brianbanton.com
Web: brianbanton.com

Brian Banton is a graphic designer based in Toronto, Canada. He holds a Bachelor of Design from the Ontario College of Art and Design (now OCADU) in Toronto and a Master of Design from York University. He has worked for some of Canada's most renowned design firms, including The Office of Gilbert Li and Underline Studio.

Caitlin Workman

Location: Kansas City, MO, USA
Email: cworkman.design@gmail.com
Web: www.caitlinworkman.com

Caitlin Workman is a multidisciplinary designer working in Kansas City, Missouri. She designs with the premise that forward thinking and experimentation are the keys to changing perception of the public view. She recently graduated from the University of Kansas and has a BFA in Visual Communication with an emphasis in Graphic Design. She is currently working at DMH, a hybrid design and advertising firm in Kansas City.

Chattermark

Location: Cherbourg-Octeville, France
Tel: 00 33 (0)2 33 52 22 29
Web: www.chattermark.fr; www.behance.net/chattermark

Stéphane Pouzencormer, a former fighter pilot, founded Chattermark in 2009 in Cherbourg, France. Steffi Marie joined the studio two years later. Steffi finished graphic design studies at UCCA, UK and La Cambre, Belgium. Cross-generational and cultural exchanges, valued experience, and understanding of all domains leads chattermark beyond clients' expectations through an approach that is as creative as it is rational: "Illusionists do not compete with designers only because magic has limits!"

Chiara Cavagion

Location: Torino, Italy
Email: c.cavagion@gmail.com
Web: www.behance.net/ccavagion

Chiara Cavagion was born in Rivoli in 1989. She attended a scientific high school, has a bachelor degree from Polytechnic of Turin, and now holds a Doctorate in Graphic and Virtual Design. In 2012 she completed a short internship at London's design firm "Method Two," which was followed by a six-month collaboration with design and architecture studio "Bodà." She is now a freelance graphic designer while maintaining her textile business.

Chloe Lassen

Location: Wellington, New Zealand
Tel: 0273549825
Web: www.behance.net/chloelassen

Chloe Lassen has been studying Graphic Design for the past six years. Based in Wellington, New Zealand, she has just completed her Bachelor of Visual Communication Design (First Class Honours) at Massey University. She is currently in the process of publishing her first book *Hear Our Voices*. She has a strong passion for typography, editorial design, transformational and experiential marketing theory as well as painting.

CR-eate

Location: Miami, FL, USA
Tel: 786 307 1767
Web: www.cr-eate.com

CR-eate is the home of the multidisciplinary work of Camilo Rojas, currently based in Miami. Camilo Rojas works with agencies, design studios, and startups on projects across a wide range of disciplines, from identity and brand development, to friendly web design, typographic treatments, print, packaging, environmental, digital, street art and bespoke commissions. Her collaborative, idea-driven process strives for simplicity, playfulness and craftsmanship.

Cristina Vila Nadal

Location: Barcelona, Spain
Tel: +34 620 43 42 59
Web: www.cristinavilanadal.es

Restless, curious, and meticulous, Cristina Vila Nadal is a designer with an analogue approach in an increasingly digital world. She studies graphic design at Eina, University School of Design and Art of Barcelona. After her stay at Barcelona studio Lo Siento, the design movement in Monterrey piqued her interest. A dreamer, she is fond of reading, plants, and unwinding with Italian mafia movies and pasta.

DADADA Studio

Location: Vilnius, Lithuania
Tel: 370 62 62 8660; 370 61 54 1101
Web: dadadastudio.eu

DADADA Studio is a Vilnius-based design and photography studio. Photographer Dalia Jankunaite and designer Martynas Birskys established it in 2005. The challenge for DADADA Studio is to provide a boutique image-creation service and enjoyable creative process. That is probably the reason why they like to say, "We still don't know who we are and what we do."

Daniel Reed

Location: Manchester, UK
Email: danielreeddesigns@gmail.com
Web: behance.net/danielreed

Daniel Reed is an artist, designer, musician, music producer, sound sampler, and typographer living in South Manchester. His approach to work is simple: He takes the time to understand the clients' aims and whom they are trying to reach, then uses his experience to create memorable, relevant work. He uses thoughtful and apposite responses to the needs of the brief, using original ideas that sensitively play with the subject matter.

D'Apostrophe, Firenze

Location: Florence, Italy
Email: mail@d-apostrophe.com
Web: www.d-apostrophe.com

Founded in Florence in 2009, D'Apostrophe is a studio that specializes in product, interior, exhibit/installation, art direction, corporate identity, editorial and web design. The founders, Donatello D'Angelo and Cosimo Damiano D'Aprile, share not only the eponymous punctuation mark in their surnames, but above all, a love of precision design across a wide range of fields.

Doradora Design Studio

Location: Buenos Aires, Argentina
Email: dolores@doradora.com.ar
Web: www.doradora.com.ar

Doradora is a young, full-service design studio founded by the sister duo Dolores (Graphic Designer) and María Oliver (Industrial Designer), based in Buenos Aires, Argentina. They work in all areas of graphic and industrial design, such as branding, corporate identity, editorial, product design, packaging, art direction, typography, web design, 3D modeling, and furniture design. They are involved in the whole design process, from the idea to the result, complementing their disciplines and skills.

Eduardo Rodrigues

Location: Matosinhos, Portugal
Tel: +351 918 871 196
Web: www.behance.net/eduardo; rodrigues

Typography enthusiast Eduardo Rodrigues was born in 1988 in Barcelos, Portugal. He graduated in 2013 in Graphic Design from School of Arts and Design in Matosinhos. He's now based in Oporto, working as creative designer in a collective called Another Collective.

Eugenia Mello

Location: Buenos Aires, Argentina
Tel: 0054 11 4780 3522
Web: www.behance.net/eu

Eugenia Mello lives in Buenos Aires, where she recently obtained a Graphic Design degree from the University of Buenos Aires. She still goes to university, where she is now an assistant teacher in two annual courses. She is highly interested in design, art, illustration, and all forms of visual representation. She was recognized as a semifinalist in the 2013 Adobe Design Achievement Awards in the Print-Communications category.

Federica Artuffo

Location: Cuneo, Italy
Email: f.artuffo@virgilio.it
Web: www.behance.net/FedericaArtuffo

Federica Artuffo was born in Alba in 1990. She attended a scientific high school. Her bachelor-degree's name is "Progetto grafico e virtual." During university, she completed an internship as a graphic designer for La Commerciale S.r.l., a typography studio based in Alba. She holds a Doctorate of Graphic Design from Polytechnic of Turin. She now lives in Milano, pursuing a Master in Business Design at the Domus Academy University.

Federico Kanno

Location: Buenos Aires, Argentina.
Tel: +54911 15 6874 1879
Web: be.net/federicokanno

Federico Kanno is a young 22-year-old graphic design student from Buenos Aires, Argentina. After finishing high school, he started studying graphic design at University of Buenos Aires; a year later he started working for advertising agencies focusing on motion graphic design. He is currently working freelance, seeking to expand his knowledge in the wonderful world of design.

Fernanda Cuenca

Location: Buenos Aires, Argentina
Tel: +5411 1569277161
Fax: +5411 47605779
Web: cargocollective.com/fernandacuenca

Fernanda Cuenca, born in 1989 in Argentina, is a graphic design student currently based in Buenos Aires. She started her professional career at a German digital agency, where she mostly worked doing editorial, web/app layout, storyboards, style-frames, and interactive design for global prime brands. She is very infatuated with graphic arts, and is always looking for new ways of communication.

Fernando Torres Rojo

Location: Pachuca, Mexico
Tel: +52 7717466196
Web: www.behance.net/Fernando-Torres-Rojo

Fernando Torres Rojo is a graphic designer based in Pachuca, Mexico. He has been collaborating on different editorial projects, like Revista Combo, and Revista CUADRO, where he has developed as graphic editor, and art director. His illustrations are the result of a mix of cultures, myths, and legends of many countries, and have been published in Pachuca and Mexico City.

Fever Chu

Location: Hong Kong & Shenzhen, China
Tel: (852) 9340 3184
Web: be.net/feverchu

Fever Chu studied Digital Graphic Communication at Hong Kong Baptist University. After graduating from college, he joined ChinaStylus and developed a wide range of skills. In 2011, he joined one of Hong Kong's leading design companies, Kan & Lau Design Consultants. He then founded his own design studio, Uneven College, in 2012. Uneven College provides radical ideas, rational solutions, and playful design experiences.

Firebelly Design

Location: Chicago, IL, USA
Tel: 773 489 3200
Web: firebellydesign.com

Firebelly is committed to cultivating connections between human beings and ideas, inspiring conscious thought and action. As early advocates for socially responsible design, they pioneered an ethic that values honesty, empathy, and Good Design for Good Reason™. Firebelly relies on their intention, intellect and instinct to guide them as they build effective communication tools that encourage conversation and engagement in and across communities to induce positive social change.

Gen Design Studio

Location: Braga, Portugal
Tel: +351 253 217 900
Web: www.gen.pt

Gen Design Studio is a company dedicated to the development of graphic, product, environmental, and web design and illustration. Placing great emphasis on project methodologies, they see design as a corporative emancipation discipline. With this strategic design perspective in mind, they're constantly aware of the world around them, predicting future scenarios and programming lines of sustainable action.

Hadid Windoro

Location: Bandung, Indonesia
Tel: +6285 722 253 114
Web: be.net/hadidwindoro

Hadid Windoro is an international relations student at Padjadjaran University. He pursues his dream to be a great graphic designer by learning it all on his own. Since 2010 he has been actively working on projects from various clients ranging from layout to branding. In 2012 his design was listed in the Top 51 Selected Works by Nirmana Awards. In 2013, he worked as a layout designer for one of Indonesia's leading newspapers, *Kompas*.

Hiba Jaroudi

Location: Beirut, Lebanon
Tel: 00971502881781; 009613221159
Email: hibajaroudi@gmail.com
Web: hibajaroudi.com

Born and raised in Beirut, Hiba graduated from the Lebanese American University with a BA in Graphic Design. After 13 years of experience, she was able to develop her own brand identity. She began her career in 2000 as a graphic designer; today she is an established digital artist with a passion to create vibrant art pieces ranging from collage on canvas to home furniture, accessories, and various customized pieces that reflect the client's unique interests, the family's city or even the client's personal visual journey.

HOAX

Location: Utrecht, Netherlands
Tel: +31 0 30 280 00 68
Web: www.hoaxhoaxhoax.com

HOAX was established by Bram Buijs, Steven van der Kaaij, and Sven Gerhardt. It's a graphic design agency based in Utrecht, the Netherlands. Its members' combined love for typography, materials, and experimentation made them decide to start working together under a shared name. They're aiming to create a certain way of working, which results in unique visual translations, rather than repeating themselves visually and conceptually.

Human After All

Location: London, UK
Tel: +44 20 7729 7694
Web: humanafterall.co.uk

Human After All is a creative agency that works across print, digital, social media and events, creating things people want to be a part of. They collaborate with some of the world's most forward-thinking organizations, including Google, World Economic Forum, Adidas, and Volkswagen, using their passion for design and communications to help clients achieve their objectives.

Ines Aryaniputri

Location: Jakarta, Indonesia
Tel: +62 899 1147 147
Web: www.be.net/inesaryaniputri

Ines Aryaniputri is a multidisciplinary graphic designer based in Jakarta, Indonesia. She began studying graphic design in 2010, and got the Best Design Student Award from UniSadhuGuna International College in 2012. She also holds a Bachelor of Honors degree from North Umbria University, United Kingdom. Since college, she has been working as a freelance designer, specializing in branding and publishing. In 2013, she began working in one of Indonesia's notable graphic design firms, LeBoYe.

Irene Fucci

Location: Turin, Italy
Email: f.iris@libero.it
Web: www.behance.net/irenefucci

Irene Fucci was born in Turin, Italy, in 1990. In 2009, she graduated with honors from high school, where she studied foreign languages; she then graduated from the Polytechnic of Turin in 2013 with a Bachelor of Graphic Design. During her undergraduate studies, Irene started working as a freelance graphic designer and portrait photographer, and became the official photographer of "6 come noi," a musician in Italy.

Ivorin Vrkaš

Location: Zagreb, Croatia
Tel: +38598224835
Web: www.ivorin.me; www.rationalinternational.net

Ivorin Vrkaš is a designer and visual artist from Zagreb, Croatia. He started his professional career working for Bunch, first as an intern and then a designer, while at the same time finishing his degree at the Zagreb School of Design. He has won a number of international awards for his design, including a Red Dot Communication Award, Magdalena Grand Prix, and a gold from International Design Award. In 2012, he and Bojan Opačak founded Rational International, a creative communications collective.

Ivy Zheyu Chen

Location: New York, NY, USA
Email: ivyzychen@gmail.com
Web: www.ivyzy.com

Ivy Zheyu Chen is a visual communicator based in NY with experience in branding, packaging, motion graphics, and user interface design. Ivy loves experimenting with graphics, simple forms and bright colors.

Janick Neundorf

Location: Stuttgart, Germany
Tel: +49 177 4571792
Web: www.apgrate.com

Janick Neundorf is a young graphic designer based in Stuttgart, Germany. He found his passion for great design at the age of fourteen, and from then on constantly improved his skills and knowledge. In 2010, he founded Apgrate Design, a one-man agency. Besides working for his company, he has been part of several agencies based in Germany and Switzerland, such as Strichpunkt, Duplex Design, and LSDK.

Jann de Vries

Location: Aachen, Germany
Email: kontakt@min-style.de
Web: www.min-style.de

Jann de Vries is a passionate graphic, communications, and web designer from Germany who specializes in minimal and functional design.

JKwan Design

Location: Hong Kong, China
Tel: +852 6976 7656
Web: www.jkwan.hk

The website www.jkwan.hk is the personal portfolio of Jason Kwan, a Hong Kong-based designer and amateur photographer. Jason has been working professionally for years on creative projects from identity, typography and poster design, to creative aspects of various forms of printed matters. Every piece of the 26-year-old's achievements dutifully demonstrates his unique eye for design, a vigilant sense for detail, and occasionally, a stubborn determination.

Jonathan Key

Location: New York, NY, USA
Email: Jonathangkey@gmail.com
Web: www.jonathangkey.com

Jonathan Key is a graduate of the Rhode Island School of Design, where he received the Bachelor of Fine Art degree in Graphic Design. He thoroughly enjoys the act of designing and making books, poster design, photography, painting, and theatrical light design. He is interested in exploring the boundaries between typography, theatre, theatre performance, and music intertwined with personal narrative. He enjoys telling stories, and currently lives and works in New York.

Joshua Elliff

Location: Bradford, UK
Tel: +44 (0) 7928152845
Web: www.joshuaelliff.co.uk

Joshua Elliff is a designer from West Yorkshire in northern England. He's passionate about engaging communication and has a keen eye for unusual ideas. His design ethos is based on the principles of bravery and playfulness, and he is focused on the social role design can play.

Ju Lee

Location: San Francisco, CA, USA
Tel: 213 505 8127
Web: www.juseoklee.com

Ju Lee was born in Seoul, South Korea. Now, he lives in the United States and is building the future of graphic design branding. Lee learned how to create communication programs that turn heads and grab hearts everywhere; he learned from past experiences. He fervently applies his creativeness to nurture environmental and social causes and helps organizations with sustainability at their core to thrive.

Kalina Możdżyńka

Location: Warsaw, Poland
Email: kalina.mozdzynska@gmail.com; kalina@grafaktura.com
Web: www.be.net/KalinaMozdzynska; www.grafaktura.com

Kalina Możdżyńska is a graphic designer with an artistic background, co-owner of a design studio Grafaktura, and a silkscreen workshop SITO. Her clients include Red Bull, National Theatre in Warsaw, Institut Polonais Paris. She specializes in visual identity, posters, and editorial design, especially for cultural institutions.

Kissmiklos (Miklós Kiss)

Location: Budapest, Hungary
Email: kissmiklos@kissmiklos.com
Web: www.kissmiklos.com

Miklós Kiss is a designer and visual artist. Currently architecture, design, and graphic design are his fields of work. There is an outstanding aesthetic quality and strong artistic approach characterizing his implementations. His fine artworks define his work, just as the individual perceptional corporate identity designs and graphics created under his name.

Kolektiv Studio

Location: Prague, Czech Republic
Tel: +420 608 625 012; +420 723 840 517
Web: www.facebook.com/Kolektiv.studio; www.behance.net/Kolektiv

Kolektiv Studio was set up by Lukáš Kijonka and Michal Krůl. They focus on concept, graphic design, typography, and illustration.

Lead82

Location: Budapest, Hungary
Tel: +36 20 430 0276
Web: www.lead82.com

Lead82 is an open creative community, which was established in 2007 by Hungarian graphic designers. From the beginning, the team dealt with cultural and museum projects, primarily creating the *MúzemCafé* magazine (the magazine of the Hungarian Museum of Fine Arts), albums, exhibition catalogues, books, and online interfaces. Lead82 is multiple-certificated by international design awards, such as European Design Award, Creativity International Award (USA); in 2013 they won a Bronze Cube at 92nd Art Directors Club.

Lorem Ipsum Studio

Location: Belgrade, Serbia
Tel: +38163 72 62 045
Web: www.loremipsum.rs

Lorem Ipsum is an independent design studio based in Belgrade, Serbia. They specialize in graphic design, typography, and illustration. Lorem Ipsum emerged out of the need to rethink design out of the lifestyle context, as far removed from the logic of market as possible. Their projects question notions, concepts, practices, and tendencies in contemporary design. Nemanja Jehlicka and Nikola Zmajevic founded Lorem Ipsum studio.

Luca Fontana

Location: Milan, Italy
Tel: +39 340 33 00 595
Web: www.behance.net/lucafontana

Luca Fontana is a young graphic designer born in Belluno, Italy. He specializes in brand image and graphic design. In 2008 after getting a diploma in Art direction at Accademia di Comunicazione (Milan), he developed an eye more focused on the typography and graphic elements, and decided to become a graphic designer. From 2009 till 2013 he worked at BBDO in Milan as a graphic designer; currently he is working as a freelancer.

Mar Borrajo Valls

Location: Barcelona, Spain
Tel: 669 934 982
Web: www.marbv.com

Mar Borrajo Valls came to Barcelona from Tarragona in 2003 and has been practicing graphic design for eight years. She has a BFA degree from the University of Barcelona, and a master's degree in Typography from Eina School and University of Barcelona. She also works as a graphic design professor in Eserp, Barcelona.

Mariana Alcobia

Location: Loures, Portugal
Tel: +351 91 700 26 18
Web: www.behance.net/marianaalcobia

Mariana Alcobia is a 22-year-old Portuguese graphic designer, born and raised in Lisbon. She has a degree in Communication Design from the Faculty of Fine Arts of the University of Lisbon (FBAUL) and has had the opportunity of studying as an exchange student in Ghent (Belgium) at The Royal Academy of Fine Arts (KASK). Mariana is passionate about book design and calligraphy. She is currently working as an intern at Designways, a rising Portuguese graphic design studio.

Marina Lavrova

Location: Moscow, Russia
Tel: +7 903 610 42 12
Web: be.net/marinalavrova

Marina Lavrova is an independent freelance designer specializing in graphic, web design, identity, and typography design.

Martin Sitta

Location: Chicago, IL, USA
Tel: 708-439-7429
Web: www.martinsitta.com

Born and raised in the Czech Republic, Martin Sitta is currently based in Chicago. Martin began as an amateur photographer and eventually started experimenting with painting and graphic design. Today, he is a creative designer of many dimensions. Martin's other expertise includes typography, packaging, editorial design, and food photography. His endless pursuit of original work allows him to stand out visually and fundamentally with unique yet timeless solutions for his clients.

Marton Borzak

Location: Copenhagen, Denmark
Tel: +4542268121; +36702365642
Web: www.martonborzak.com

Marton Borzak is a Hungarian graphic designer and art director currently based in Copenhagen. He studied at the

Hungarian University of Fine Arts and The Royal Danish Academy of Fine Arts, School of Design. During his career he has worked with national and international clients. The range of clients spans from small startup companies to banks. He always tries to work with different people to keep his passion in this profession alive.

Massimo Künstler

Location: Rome, Italy
Email: massimo@kunstler.it
Web: www.kunstler.it

Massimo Künstler is an independent multimedia designer based in Rome, Italy, providing quality solutions for brand strategy, creative identity, and interactive design. His work is enhanced and supported by a network of independent professionals specializing in corporate, print, web, mobile, and social media.

Matilde Digmann Designs

Location: Copenhagen, Denmark
Tel: +45 27 82 66 00
Web: www.matildedigmann.dk

Matilde Digmann is a Copenhagen-based art director and illustrator, working within the fields of culture, fashion, and art. Matilde holds a master's degree in Art History and Media Science as well as her degree as Graphic Designer. She has been practicing graphic design, art direction, curation, and illustration for nearly a decade, and is running her own studio from the wonderful neighborhood "Nørrebro" in Copenhagen.

Matt Willey

Location: London, UK
Email: mail@mattwilley.co.uk
Web: www.mattwilley.co.uk

Matt Willey graduated from Central Saint Martins in 1997. Having gained valuable experience at a handful of small design companies, he joined the internationally acclaimed studio Frost Design, later becoming Creative Director. In 2005 he co-founded Studio8 Design with Zoë Bather. Matt is on the board of the Editorial Design Organization, Vice Chairman of The Typographic Circle and visiting lecturer at Skolen for Visuel Kommunikation in Denmark.

Matthieu Cordier

Location: Besançon, France
Tel: +33 (0)6.25.50.21.21
Web: matthieucordier.tumblr.com

Matthieu Cordier is a freelance graphic designer living in

Besançon, France. He graduated with a DNSEP (equal to master's degree diploma) with highest honors from the Graphic Design Department of the Higher Institute of Fine Arts in Besançon. He focuses principally on print design (books, flyers, posters, identities and the like) but also works on digital design and sound design.

Moodley brand identity

Location: Graz, Austria
Tel: 0043 316 822922 0
Fax: 0043 316 822922 22
Web: www.moodley.at

Moodley brand identity is an owner-led, award-winning strategic design agency with offices in Vienna and Graz. Since 1999, moodley has worked together with customers to develop corporate and product brands that live, breathe, and grow. Moodley believes that its key contribution is to analyze complex requirements and develop simple, smart solutions with emotional appeal — whether it's for corporate start-up, product launch or brand positioning.

OK200

Location: Amsterdam, Netherlands
Tel: +31 (0)6 412 411 47
Web: www.ok200.nl

OK200 is an Amsterdam-based graphic design studio founded by Mattijs de Wit and Koen Knevel in 2010. The name OK200 comes from a server response code, which means: "Your request has succeeded." OK200 is a personal, headstrong, fast, and authentic graphic design studio. They make no distinction between working for a big corporate company or a cultural institution. OK200 has experience in working on various projects, from websites to magazines, to identities, and to whatever you request.

Olga Angelaki

Location: London, UK
Tel: +44 7453 286983
Web: www.olgaangelaki.com;
www.behance.net/olgaangelaki

Olga Angelaki is a London-based designer who has been working across different disciplines and media since 2007. She loves chocolate and sunny days, art galleries, and big challenges. Having an undeniable passion for printed matter, bold colors and lomography, Olga has been wandering around to draw inspiration from anything that catches her eye.

Omar Reda

Location: Riyad, Saudi Arabia
Tel: 00966 55 733 7335
Web: www.omarreda.net

Born in Tripoli in 1984, Lebanon, Omar Reda graduated with honors in Graphic Design from Notre Dame University. Omar is a member of the International Society of Typographic Design, London. He has worked in different international companies (Y&R, Intermarkets and TBWA\RAAD) where he was the art director for many key clients in Saudi Arabia including Almarai, Unilever, Al Rajhi Bank, Riyad Bank, and others.

Paloma Ernd | Design & Illustration

Location: Munich, Germany
Email: hi@palomaernd.de
Web: www.palomaernd.de

Paloma Ernd is a young freelance designer based in Munich, Germany. Since 2011, she has been working on a wide range of different projects, such as experimental work for local bands, magazines, clubs, and small businesses, as well as corporate and editorial projects for companies. She specializes in graphics, illustration, and typography.

Patrycja Dulnik

Location: Warsaw, Poland
Email: patrycja.dulnik@gmail.com
Web: behance.net/patrycja_dulnik

Patrycja Dulnik is a freelance graphic designer based in Warsaw, Poland. She graduated with honors from The Academy of Fine Arts in Warsaw. From an early age she was interested in fields of graphics, illustration, and editorial design. She recently collaborated with one of the top brand design studios, Element One. This studio combines the features of an advertising agency, publishing house, and design studio, and it specializes in visual publishing. The studio has won many prestigious awards.

Pau Alekumsalaam

Location: Barcelona, Spain
Tel: +34 628 734 187
Web: www.pauerr.com

Pau Alekumsalaam is a Spanish designer. His research is based on the areas of graphic arts and new media technology. He graduated Magna Cum Laude with a BA in Graphic Design from Elisava School of Design and Engineering. He has worked for several agencies, such as Cline Davis & Mann, Bubblegum and Do not disturb. In 2012 he won a European award for developing an experimental cartography project in collaboration with Istituto Europeo di Design, in Milan.

Ramon Lenherr

Location: St. Gallen, Switzerland
Email: ramon@ramonlenherr.ch
Web: www.ramonlenherr.ch

Ramon Lenherr is a graphic designer working in St. Gallen, Switzerland.

Rasmus und christin

Location: Graz, Austria
Email: wir@rasmusundchristin.de
Web: www.rasmusundchristin.de

Rasmus und christin are graphic designers from Germany, currently working in an interdisciplinary agency in Austria. They are passionate about book design, magazines, and brand identities. Their ambition is to simplify and clear complicated forms and structures, and create unique conceptual work with a focus on typographic solutions.

Ricardo Vieira

Location: Cardiff, Wales, UK
Tel: 075 8268 5672
Web: www.vieira.com.pt

Ricardo Vieira was born in 1990 in Portimão, Portugal. A multidisciplinary graphic designer and illustrator, he focuses on branding, advertising and illustration. With the professional experience gained from working as a graphic designer, he developed the skill to accomplish any brief, giving the client a satisfying result of creativity and functionality.

Romeo Vidner

Location: Copenhagen, Denmark
Tel: +45 7020 9890
Web: www.re-public.com

Romeo Vidner is a Swedish designer and was educated at The Graphic Arts Institute of Denmark and School of Arts and Communication in Sweden. He has been practicing graphic design in Copenhagen for nine years. Since 2006 he has worked at Re-public. Romeo has been honored with several international design awards and has been a jury-member of the Danish design competition, Creative Circle Awards.

Ronan Kelly

Location: Dublin, Ireland
Tel: 0857270737
Web: www.ronankellydesign.com

Ronan Kelly is a recent graduate of Design for Visual Communications at IADT, Dublin. Having grown up in Spain, Ronan now lives in Dublin. He participated in the Three x 3 internship through summer of 2014. He has been practicing freelance graphic design for three years and has completed projects for a variety of clients in the fields of music, art, and architecture.

Sam van Straaten

Location: Cape Town, South Africa
Tel: 0833592837
Email: hello@samvanstraaten.com
Web: www.samvanstraaten.com

Sam van Straaten was born and raised in South Africa. After completing a degree with honors in Visual Communication Design at Stellenbosch University in 2009, he moved to Cape Town, where he has been practicing design as a full-time career. He currently works in advertising and freelances in his free time.

Samantha Fine

Location: Chicago, USA
Email: samantha.l.fine@gmail.com
Web: samfinedesign.com

Samantha Fine is a designer in Chicago, Illinois. She graduated in 2012 from the University of Kansas with a BFA in Visual Communication. Samantha spent time studying graphic design at the Fachhochschule (University of Applied Sciences) in Trier, Germany. She currently works in Chicago at a production company, working primarily in motion graphic design.

Sawdust

Location: London, UK
Tel: + 44 (0) 20 7739 9787
Web: madebysawdust.co.uk

Sawdust is the award-winning creative partnership of Rob Gonzalez and Jonathan Quainton. They are an independent design duo based in London, UK. The disciplines they work in include custom typography, image-making, identity, and art direction across music, art, culture, fashion, corporate and advertising sectors.

Scandinavian DesignLab

Location: Copenhagen, Denmark
Tel: +45 702 708 06
Web: www.scandinaviandesignlab.com

Scandinavian DesignLab is an independent design agency based in Copenhagen, Denmark with representation in Shanghai, China. Identity is the core business with the vision of building corporate souls that actually identify and distinguish, and envisioning product brands that connect with the target, build preferences, and win the battle at the moment of truth.

Sebastián Ruiz Díaz

Location: Buenos Aires, Argentina
Tel: 54 011 4988 1329
Web: www.sebastianruizdiaz.com

Sebastián is a graphic designer based in Buenos Aires who has studied at the prestigious Faculty of Architecture, Design and Urbanism, University of Buenos Aires. He admires the great designers of all times, works independently on different projects and in different areas of design, and deeply loves what he does.

Sergei Kudinov

Location: Moscow, Russia
Tel: +7 926 326 47 22
Web: be.net/kudinov

Sergei Kudinov is a freelance designer and art director working and living in Moscow, Russia. He also worked as a leading designer in Condé Nast Russia Publishing House, and Sinaxis Publishing Company.

Stefan Zimmermann

Location: Eschweiler, Germany
Email: kontakt@deszign.de
Web: www.deszign.de

Stefan Zimmermann received his BA degree in Communication Design in 2012 from the FH Aachen, University of Applied Sciences, Faculty of Design. During his studies he focused primarily on the areas of corporate design, typography and web design. At this time of this publication, he is working on his master's degree in Communication Design and Product Design at the FH Aachen.

Stephanie Passul

Location: Wuppertal, Germany
Email: mail@stephaniepassul.de
Web: www.stephaniepassul.de

Stephanie Passul is a freelance graphic designer focused on editorial design, typography, and art direction. Her work includes print media, such as magazines, books, and posters, as well as visual identities, websites, and installations. Stephanie's work is always content-related, based on a conceptual approach and a clear, bold visual language.

Tomato Košir

Location: Kranj, Slovenia (EU)
Tel: +386 41 260 979
Email: tomato@tomatokosir.com
Web: www.tomatokosir.com

Tomato Košir is a young designer, awarded by both Art Directors Club New York and Type Directors Club New York. He obtained his MA in 2007, and was an assistant professor at Academy of Art and Design, Ljubljana. He served as President of the Fourth Biennial of Slovene Visual Communications 2009. He is the founder of TypeClinic — international type design workshops — and a co-organizer of the First Festival of Letters, Ljubljana.

Toormix

Location: Barcelona, Spain
Tel: 0034 93 486 90 90
Web: www.toormix.com

Toormix is a creative studio started in Barcelona in 2000, and directed by Oriol Armengou and Ferran Mitjans. They specialize in design and brand identity. They face their projects with a clear strategic and conceptual vision, always looking for innovative visual approaches. They work within their atelier, a parallel space oriented towards research, thinking, and their own projects.

Trapped in Suburbia

Location: Hague, Netherlands
Tel: +31 070 389 0858
Web: www.trappedinsuburbia.com

Trapped in Suburbia's designs are focused on the experience of the audience; therefore the designers choose the medium that has the most impact. This forces them to be interdisciplinary and challenges their talents and knowledge in an exciting manner. They aim to stay open-minded, seek out for experiments, and play.

Valentina D'Efilippo

Location: London, UK
Email: valentina.defilippo@gmail.com
Web: www.valentinadefilippo.co.uk

Valentina D'Efilippo is a multi-disciplinary designer with an appetite for creativity and innovation — across all formats and media. After studying industrial design in Italy, she moved to London and gained a post-graduate degree in graphic design. She has worked with a number of leading agencies, contributing to award-winning campaigns for global brands looking to sell more cars, oil and beer. Valentina founded London-based Italika Design in 2011.

Vincent Schwenk

Location: Munich, Germany
Email: hi@vincentschwenk.de
Web: vincentschwenk.de

Vincent Schwenk is a 25-year-old designer from Munich, Germany. He graduated in 2012 with a BA in Communication Design. He is currently working as a freelancer for national and international clients.

Violaine et Jérémy

Location: Paris, France
Tel: +33 6 59 45 78 58
Web: violaineetjeremy.fr; behance.net/violaineetjeremy

Violaine and Jérémy are together in life and at work. Violaine Orsoni used to be a production director for advertising agencies in Paris. Jérémy Schneider has always been a natural illustrator and a graphic designer. In 2009, he brilliantly graduated from the French public graphic design school, EPSAA. They decided to begin their own adventure in 2011. Since then, they have worked with orchestras, fashion magazines, cultural institutions and more.

Vivian Lobenwein

Location: Florianópolis, Brazil
Tel: 55 48 9134.5858
Web: www.behance.net/vivianlobenwein

Vivan Lobenwein graduated in 2006 from the State University of Santa Catarina. While still in college, Vivian started doing projects for magazines and books; she has specialized in publishing for the last nine years. Recently she has become part of a creative and collaborative project that serves multiple clients (small, medium and large companies), mainly in the fashion market. Her portfolio also includes book design, custom magazines, fashion catalogs, and visual identity.

Wildan Ilham

Location: Jakarta, Indonesia
Email: wildwildan13@gmail.com
Web: behance.net/wildan

Wildan Ilham is a student in the Visual Communication Design Department of Bina Nusantara University, whose focus is on print design, illustration, and typography. In between his studies, he contributes as an artist and illustrator to *Titik Dua* magazine.

Wolfgang Landauer

Location: Simbach, Germany
Email: buero.wolfgang@gmail.com
Web: www.be.net/wolfganglandauer;
www.wolfganglandauer.de

Wolfgang Landauer has been practicing graphic design for six years. He is currently completing his studies for a master's degree in Visual Communication at the University of Applied Sciences in Mainz, after receiving his BA in Visual Communication at the University of Applied Sciences in Würzburg.

Zoran Lucić

Location: Bijeljina, Bosnia and Herzegovina
Email: zoranlucicdva@gmail.com
Web: www.behance.net/zoranlucic

Zoran Lucić was born in Šabac, Serbia (former Yugoslavia) and grew up in Domaljevac, Bosnia and Herzegovina, and Hungary. He studied graphics and design at University of Bijeljina, B&H, and, although his first love was sculpting, he later discovered an affinity for typography. He now lives in Bijeljina and works as a freelance designer.